Silo
Country

a true story

Silo Country
a true story

AMANDA ROBIN LARCHER

AMBASSADOR INTERNATIONAL
GREENVILLE, SOUTH CAROLINA & BELFAST, NORTHERN IRELAND

www.ambassador-international.com

Silo Country
A True Story

© 2013 by Amanda Robin Larcher

ISBN: 978-1-62020-202-9
eISBN: 978-1-62020-300-2

Cover design and typesetting: Matthew Mulder
E-book conversion: Anna Riebe

AMBASSADOR INTERNATIONAL
Emerald House
427 Wade Hampton Blvd.
Greenville, SC 29609, USA
www.ambassador-international.com

AMBASSADOR BOOKS
The Mount
2 Woodstock Link
Belfast, BT6 8DD, Northern Ireland, UK
www.ambassadormedia.co.uk

The colophon is a trademark of Ambassador

To my family which nurtured my soul.

CONTENTS

PROLOGUE

BUCKLE UP! YOU ARE ABOUT TO land in French territory. If you are French, you know what to expect. If you are not, you might have heard some things about my country. Americans are especially gracious and fond of their old allies. However, when they come to visit, some return home puzzled by the cold welcome they received. *Do the French still love the Americans?* Africans might take the way they are treated more personally. *Is it racism?*

Outsiders—adults in particular—are tempted to ask the question: *why do the French act that way?* While they try to sort out diverse and complex motivations, they barely survive the culture shock.

Trying to explain the French psychology would take more than this humble prologue. How can I help young readers understand the French experience?

Maybe by telling them Amanda, as a French girl, struggled also within her own culture. So did a number of her schoolmates for that matter.

Her story is neither a judgment nor an attempt to absolve her society. It is a view from within. I do not want readers to think Amanda had all the answers, or most of her answers were even right.

Instead, I will have accomplished a purpose if, while reading, one stops and asks practical questions such as:

- *What would I have done in her place?*

If you have inherited strong family values, ask a deeper question:

- *What should I have done, in her place? Or, what would be a better way to handle the situation?*

If you can come up with better answers, you will be ready for a better landing.

What helped me most growing up in France were the family conversations that took place around the supper table. My father would say: "This situation might come up again. Get ready for the next time."

The idea is to face the French challenge, rather than wonder why there is a French challenge.

As you set out on this adventure, keep a couple of hints in mind:

- The French are first and foremost human beings, and all that entails.
- Under their hard shell, there is a heart, often craving for true friendship.

ACKNOWLEDGMENTS

THE FOLLOWING PEOPLE HAVE BEEN A tremendous encouragement as I become a published author:

A few years ago, author, Dr. Howard Vos, told me: "You should write!" I still remember his declaration.

My parents and brother loved reading the first French manuscript. That was encouraging!

Retired editor, Bob Delancy, kindly walked me—step-by-step—through the editing of my first translation of *Silo Country* into U.S. English. Bob, I learned so much from you.

Author, Terence Sherwood, asked me: "Why don't you publish? It's not that difficult."

Author, Dianne Beale, kindly fixed my computer, and then proofread *Silo Country*. Dianne, you are so gifted!

Writer's Edge did a tremendous job to bring the manuscript to the attention of publishers.

Editor, Vanessa Suggs Wallace's insight and comments transformed the text into a professional product.

Ambassador International Publishers have made the publishing process an experience not to miss.

Many friends have prayed for this book to come to life.

I am especially thankful to each one of my four children who have showed unlimited grace and understanding to their dreaming mother.

Yes, my husband, in his own way, has been supporting me thoroughly through the whole process.

God placed gifted people along my way, and provided me with gifts. *Silo Country* is the story He weaved into my childhood. I am indebted to Him for my very life. Thank you, my Lord and Savior.

Pour moi, plus de crainte,
  De larmes, de plainte,
Pour moi, plus de crainte,
Jésus règne en mon cœur.

—Jean-Sébastien Bach (1685–1750)

A STRANGE SONG

THAT WINTER OF 1967 IN PARIS, in the suburb of Le Bourget, Amanda was nearly five years old. Since her birth the roar of the airplanes, flying at regular intervals above the capital city, made up, in part, the familiar sounds of her universe. Her father, Armand Vissac, had returned home from work. He sang heartily. Behind his back, she and her six year old brother, Jean-Baptiste (pronounced *John Bateest*), listened to the passionate words of Jean-Sébastien Bach's "Pentecost":

> "Exalte-toi mon âme,
> Entonne un chant de flammes,
> Des bienheureux, entends le chœur,
> Vois ton Jésus vainqueur."[1]

In the kitchen, their mother, Louise, sneezed. Armand went down to the cellar to stack the wood in the stove that heated the whole house while his young wife put the last touches on the evening meal. A warm smell of vegetable soup followed him to the bottom of the stairs.

---

1 Exalt yourself my soul, sing a flaming song, hear the choir of the Blessed, and see your victorious Jesus.

When he reappeared in the kitchen, he turned on the radio. Armand listened intently to the flow of words that meant nothing to the children. However, they understood when, at the table, their father shared his concern with them.

"There is a shortage of wood in the whole city of Paris," he said.

"Oui," his wife answered, "and this winter is particularly cold."

"If it continues like this, I'm afraid we'll run out of wood."

Louise quickly reached into her apron pocket as a sneezing fit shook her. She hid her pretty face in a wide, white handkerchief.

★ ★ ★

The next morning, when the two children woke up, their father had already left for work. In the middle of the day, as they joyfully played, Amanda began to sing Bach's song with a clear voice:

"Exalte-toi mon âne, enjambe un champ de flammes."[2]

Jean-Baptiste shook his head.

"Uh-uh! It's not *mon âne*; it's *mon âme*."

"*Mon âme*' doesn't mean anything," the little girl protested.

Her brother seemed embarrassed.

He replied, "Maybe; however, it's still *mon âme*."

"You always think you're right because you're the oldest! That's what!"

"I'm right because I'm right."

"Not true!" Amanda yelled.

A fight was about to start when the boy suggested, "Let's wait for Papa to come home, and then we can ask him which of us is right."

"That's a good idea!"

---

2 Exalt yourself my donkey, jump over a field in flames.

* * *

Armand came home early. He appeared in the kitchen, his arms filled with shopping bags. His children ran to welcome him.

They spoke in unison, "Papa, Papa, we want to ask you something."

Amanda, her arms stretched out, jumped to reach his arms. Their father hurriedly set the bags of food on the floor before they tumbled down.

"Now, now, what's going on?"

Jean-Baptiste explained very clearly, "When we sing your song, Amanda says, *'Mon âne,'* and I say, *'Mon âme.'* Which of us is right?"

Their father made an effort to not laugh. His daughter had only performed a little trick to exchange the word: soul against the word: donkey. He turned his back on the children, pretending to put away the food, but they waited.

When he finally turned around, he answered seriously, "Well, I suppose that for Jean-Baptiste, it is mon âme and for Amanda, it is mon âne."

"But Papa!" she protested. *"Mon âme* doesn't mean anything."

Armand thought carefully as he said, *"L'âme* is that part within us which we can't see, but which is eternal."

Amanda's eyes widened. She touched her chest.

*I **do** have a soul inside me!*

"What does eternal mean?"

"When our body dies, l'âme is the part of us that will never die, or that will live forever . . . if you wish."

"I still wonder how a soul can jump over a field in flames," she murmured.

Her father looked at her, wondering. This time, he was not sure he properly understood.

"You'll understand that later, when you are older."

She sighed.

"It's always the same. Everybody tells me I'm too little, but someday, I'll know."

"Maybe you'll have forgotten by then," he suggested.

"No, I'll never forget!" she said, determined.

THE MOUNTAINEER OF PARIS

LOUISE SNEEZED. HER HUSBAND LOOKED AT her, worried.

"Have you caught a cold?" he asked.

"I don't think so," she sighed. "I rather think it's some kind of allergy."

He frowned, and then went on, "Louise, I'm going out again right now. Today, I made a delivery along the tracks by the train station. I saw a whole pile of old railroad wood sleepers rotting under the snow. I'm going to get them before nightfall. They'll make good firewood."

"Are they likely to let you in?"

"I've already made several deliveries there. They know me."

Turning toward his son, he continued, "Get Jean-Baptiste wrapped up warmly. I'll take him along. He'll help me."

"Me, too, Papa," Amanda begged.

Her father smiled.

"Get them both wrapped up. She'll help me, too. She can hold the door."

"You are sure?" Louise asked.

"Of course, I am. If I get into trouble, at least they'll see I have a young family."

As soon as the children were bundled up, he put his young daughter in the van. Jean-Baptiste climbed up after his sister and huddled with her on the single seat.

"Let's go."

Armand worked his way skillfully through the thick Parisian traffic. Occasionally, he even drove on the sidewalk; he always avoided traffic agents, respectfully, and accidents, cautiously. Armand knew the capital city well. He was born, grew up, and did his military service in the city as a driver for the government ministers.

Amanda's eyes widened slightly with anxiety.

"Say, Papa, will a mean man stop you from taking that wood?"

Her father let go of the wheel with his right hand, reached out, and lightly stroked her black curls.

"Don't worry, Amanda. This wood doesn't belong to anyone; therefore it belongs to everybody. Les Chemins de Fer is a national company."

"I don't understand."

"I know."

They arrived at the tracks. At the entrance, a man stood watch. Armand gave him a military salute. They knew each other.

The watchman waved him on, and they drove along the railroad until Armand stopped his engine. He jumped from the vehicle.

Amanda thrust her head out the van window, and saw a huge pile of squared beams laid right before her. Rail tracks stretched as far as her eyes could see.

In the distance, men in blue clothing worked or warmed their hands at a campfire. An engine hurried to and fro between wagons.

Jean-Baptiste took his place in the back of the van. Amanda measured the distance to the ground.

"Papa, I want to get down," she implored.

Her father pulled Amanda's hood over her head, and put her down on the frozen ground.

"Don't go too far!"

"No! I'm too scared that a train might take me away. Besides, I'm going to stand watch."

Armand smiled, amused. He reached out, grabbed a sleeper, and pushed it inside the vehicle. Jean-Baptiste helped as best as he could, for his father worked fast. Amanda walked away, but quickly ran back.

"Don't stand in my way!" Armand exclaimed.

"Papa, look! A man in blue overalls is coming toward us."

Armand looked up, but he did not stop working until the man reached them. Then, he slowed down, stopped, and took off one of his gloves. He blew on his frozen fingers.

"Hi!" he shouted.

"Are you recycling?"

"Yes, sir," he answered without hesitation.

"Are you from the company?"

"I deliver merchandise here."

The overseer noticed the boy whose cheeks were pink from his effort. He caught sight of the little girl, hidden behind her father's pants, heart beating. Her two bright eyes—circled by the down of a hood from which rebellious locks escaped—drew a smile from him.

He pointed to the wood and said, "With the situation being what it is, it's a good idea. It would be a sin to let these discarded sleepers rot."

"That's exactly what I think," Armand confirmed, relieved.

"Good luck!"

The man left as suddenly as he had arrived.

"Come on, Youyoune[3]," the father exclaimed joyfully. "Get out from under my feet, will you?"

* * *

---

3 Affectionate name Armand made up for his daughter, referring to her bright eyes.

At home, Louise waited, listening for them. She recognized the sound of the engine and ran to open the gate to the courtyard. The snow fell again.

"We have wood!" Armand shouted as soon as he was out of the vehicle. "Leave the kitchen door open. I'll take it to the cellar right now."

"I'm so glad."

"Say, those who think they've invented the word recycling have invented nothing yet," he called to his wife merrily. "Ages ago, my ancestors practiced this art every day. In patois, we say: rapetassage."

"I know," she said and laughed.

Even Amanda, who was totally ignorant of that language, had heard the word.

* * *

Armand Vissac was proud of himself for having once again honored the tradition of a long line of ancestors who had their roots in Haute-Loire. For, like his original kinfolk, he never considered himself to be a Parisian. He was the son of immigrants—poor, frugal mountaineers.

In fact, faithful to his family custom, Armand had entrusted his wife with the purse. For pocket money, he only carried a ten franc coin with him.

"Just in case," he said.

However, Amanda suspected it had remained the same coin for months since he did not smoke, never went to the café, and did not read any newspaper. His greatest pleasure was to take care of his family.

His other great joy was to sing. Armand Vissac could really sing, for he had trained to become a professional singer at the Paris

Opera,[4] before his marriage.

* * *

As she stood on the doorstep, Louise looked so pretty with big, blue eyes she had inherited from her Alsatian roots. Armand felt inspired to sing a love song as he emptied the van:

> "You are so beautiful,
>   my sweet, blond angel,
> That I, with my loving lips,
> While kissing your forehead,
> Seem to be losing life.
> My youth, my lute, and my winged dreams--
> My only treasures, alas--I lay at your feet.
> You are so beautiful..."[5]

The words of the song died quickly, for the sweet, blond angel was overcome by a sneezing fit. Her big, blue eyes suddenly became watery. Armand stopped in his tracks.

"Louise," he declared solemnly, "we're going to move to the country! Maybe the air there will be better for you."

Surprised, she looked at him silently for a moment, and sniffed. Then she replied, "Maybe."

---

4   Opéra de Paris: Brilliant architectural national theater, dedicated to dance and lyric arts.

5   Vous êtes si jolie, 1896, paroles Léon Suès, musique Paul Delmet (1862–1904).

THYM IN THYMERAIS COUNTRY

A YEAR LATER, IN JANUARY 1968, the Vissac family moved to Thym, a small village in Thymerais country between the regions of Beauce and Perche. In the spring, when barley is still grass, the village appears to be nestled in a green ocean. In the summer, the farmland is covered with golden wheat. However, during the fall and winter, not a single stem stood.

This is a time when, in fair weather, one can count the church steeples scattered in the surrounding country. As far as the eye can see, they appear to be suspended between heaven and Earth.

The Vissacs now managed a grocery store directly across from the bakery. They lived on the main street halfway between the two ends of the village. Situated at one end of the village was the primary school. A bus normally picked up the children from the surrounding farms, but the village children walked to school.

The baker's children were brought up well. Perrine, the baker's daughter, kindly offered to accompany Amanda to school since the two girls were the same age.

Thierry, the baker's oldest son, was probably the tallest and strongest of the primary school. However, he was the gentlest and least aggressive of the boys. Thierry invited Jean-Baptiste to join him in a sprint to set a record time to reach the school, simply to avoid the bullying and fights that took place along the way.

That first morning a girl, who seemingly appeared from nowhere, joined Amanda and her new friend as they walked side-by-side.

"This is Laura," Perrine said.

Laura was a little, fair-haired child—rather thin and very shy—whose face appeared half hidden behind strange, thick, twisted glasses. A piece of scotch tape covered the inner side of each glass.

"And she's Amanda," continued Perrine, "a new girl."

"You have the same name as my mother," Laura exclaimed, suddenly reassured. "It's a pretty name."

"She's going to stay with us," Perrine added, "because she's afraid of getting her glasses crushed."

Amanda's eyes widened.

"What?"

"Well, yes. Don't you see how many times they've been glued back together?"

"With scotch tape?"

"No, the tape is because I have crossed eyes," Laura explained bravely.

A closer look revealed the glasses had been mangled.

"But it's thoroughly mean!" Amanda exclaimed. "Who would even think of crushing someone's glasses?"

Laura, now well at ease, informed her, "They say I have the eyes of a pig, so they knock my glasses down, just to see me squint."

"I've never seen a pig squint, and I don't see how it relates to your eyes."

"Well, it does. You see, I have brown eyes. Brown eyes, pig's eyes."

"Green eyes, viper's eyes," Perrine continued.

"Blue eyes, lover's eyes," Laura completed with a sigh.

"This is ridiculous," Amanda insisted. "Are you going to let people tell you that you have pig eyes? Just about everyone . . . here . . . has . . . brown eyes. My father tells me my eyes have the color of hazelnuts."

Laura smiled lightly.

"It's better than pig's eyes. Anyway, I'd like you to stay with me to pick up my glasses, when they crush them."

"Can't you do it yourself?"

"Well no, she can't see without glasses," Perrine retorted.

"Ah!"

"Not true," Laura protested, "I can see."

"Why don't you pick up your glasses when they fall, then?" Perrine asked, surprised.

"You know very well as soon as they see I'm going to pick them up, they are faster than me."

"You must become faster, then," Amanda encouraged.

"I'll never be able to."

"Have you ever tried?"

"No, but it's no use."

"You must try. If you see well enough, you'll succeed, and we'll help you."

As the girls talked, they walked up a good part of Grande Rue, the main street of the village. Other pupils came from side streets; groups formed.

Not far behind them, a boys' gang emerged out of the Rue des Silos, raging noisily. Amanda turned around. She did not notice Laura was holding her breath, but she saw one of the boys move out of the group and dash at them like an arrow.

He rushed to the middle of the three girls, and, quickly, reached for Laura's glasses, ripping them off her face. They landed a meter from her, leaving two big brown eyes bare, squinting.

"Quick Laura, pick up your glasses!"

"Quick . . . quick!"

Laura made an effort to concentrate her sight, bent down in the right direction, and reached out. Before she could take hold of her possession, the fireball came back, and, in front of Amanda's incredulous eyes, lightly jumped on the glasses. He continued his course without stopping. Meanwhile, the witnesses laughed.

They started to chant: "Brown eyes, pig's eyes!"

Laura's brown eyes slowly filled with tears. Anger seized Amanda.

"Who is he?" she grumbled.

"This is Joël," Perrine informed her.

"You're mean," she cried. "You did it on purpose. We're going to tell the teacher."

"The teacher won't believe you," he said. "Everyone here knows Laura doesn't take care of her glasses."

"Oh! I've seen it all and I'm going to tell."

"Do you wish to be called a tattletale?"

All the others joined in to chant:

"Cheap tattletale, who tattletales to her Godmother, her Godmother gives her little pennies to buy little goodies."[6]

"I don't care. Her glasses; you're going to pay for them!"

"Even the teacher will consider you to be a tattletale, and she won't do anything."

"If the teacher doesn't do anything, I'll tell my parents."

"If you tell, we'll beat you up, dirty Parisian."

Perrine seized Amanda by the arm, fearing her new friend would get roughed up, but she broke loose abruptly. The school was visible, and the teacher stood by the gate. Before anyone could stop her, Amanda ran resolutely to school authority. Perrine tried to drag Laura behind her with difficulty, as now the girl cried for fear of the boys' threats, if she dared to tell the truth.

"Are you the teacher?" Amanda asked, out of breath.

"I am, and who are you?"

"My name is Amanda Vissac, the new girl. Madame, this boy, Joël, knocked Laura's glasses down, and then he crushed them with his foot before our very eyes. He did it on purpose; I saw it. After, everyone says it's Laura's fault. Please, do something to stop that. He ought to pay for her glasses."

---

6 Rapporteuse à quatre chandelles, qui rapport à sa marraine, sa marraine lui donne des p'tits sous, pour ach'ter des p'tits joujous.

The teacher, surprised by her tirade, did not label the newcomer of tattletale.

"Who else could witness to that same story?" she finally asked.

"Perrine was there to try to protect her. Look, they're coming. Perrine, Laura, come quick!"

As the group got closer, Thierry and Jean-Baptiste, who had arrived earlier, joined their sisters; Joël kept his distance.

Perrine was no tattletale. When asked for the truth, she hesitated, but finally said it.

"I'll see what I can do," the teacher said, after having heard the story for the second time. "I'll try to talk to Joël's parents. They must have insurance. And you, Laura, stop crying. I won't shout at you, this time."

FAMILY COUNSEL

THAT EVENING, WHILE AMANDA SAT ON the front doorstep of their house, she saw her teacher enter the grocery store to do some errands. She got up swiftly, went into the living room, and came out in the corridor, which connected the house to the back of the shop. There, in the dark, she could hear everything said in the store.

"But she reads!" the teacher exclaimed. "I'm telling you she can read just about anything."

"This is incredible!" Louise answered, "I wonder how she could have learned."

"That's something you should ask her. She surely didn't learn just like that!"

Hidden in the darkness, Amanda smiled to herself. She waited as the entry doorbell rang to announce the teacher had left, and then she peeked out.

"Of course, I can read!" she stated.

"Amanda, you've been eavesdropping behind my back!"

"I saw the teacher come in, and I wanted to know if she would talk about me."

"Well, she did talk about you. The first thing she said when she came in was, 'It's incredible; she can read!'"

"But I thought you knew that!"

"No, I didn't. Your teacher just told me. I must say I'm really proud of you. By the way, how did you learn?"

"You taught me!"

"I never did! I tried to teach your brother, but it was rather arduous."

"Well, each time you taught him a lesson, and he hated it, I was there learning everything, behind his back. You always sent me away to play because you said I was bothering you."

"Well then, I didn't realize it. All the same, I want you to remember I don't want you to eavesdrop on the conversations that take place in the store."

"How am I ever going to learn anything if I don't listen behind doors?"

"Amanda, you like having the last word! But I don't want you to listen to what is said in the store. It's not for little girls and it's impolite! D'accord?"

"Oui, Maman. How can I learn anything that way?" she grumbled, just to have the last word, and then she hurried away.

* * *

The Vissac family was about to sit down at the supper table when Armand burst into the kitchen, a flashlight in one hand and a bottle of wine in the other. His dark locks and glasses were covered with spider webs.

"I've discovered a treasure!" he exclaimed.

They all looked at him.

"There's a supply of bottles of good wine in the cellar."

"What are we going to do with that?" Louise inquired.

"We'll sell them!"

"Meanwhile, it gave you white hair!" she teased.

"We'll try one of them when we get an opportunity."

Prior to this time, they had not yet been in the cellar. It was a very dark and spooky place. Armand moved to the kitchen sink (also used as a washbasin) to put his appearance back in order. He set the bottle on the floor, in a corner, and began to sing:

> "Quand Madelon vient nous servir à boire, sous la ton-
> nelle on frôle son jupon,
> Et chacun lui raconte une histoire, une histoire à sa
> façon, à Madelon!
> La Madelon pour nous n'est pas sévère, quand on lui
> prend, la taille et le menton,
> Elle rit, c'est tout l'mal qu'elle sait faire, Madelon,
> Madelon, Madelon!"[7]

As soon as they were all around the table, Amanda started to tell her parents about the events of the day.

"Poor Laura," she sighed, "she makes me so sad."

"Who's Laura?" her mother asked.

"The Blanchard girl! You know the lady who limps?"

"I do," her father acknowledged. "They live a little further up the street."

"Well, it's her daughter."

"They're good folks," he remarked.

"All the same, poor girl. Her parents ought to buy her another pair of glasses. They're all broken."

"You can't wear broken glasses."

"Well, they've been taped back together several times."

"She ought to learn to take care of them, I guess."

"The problem is that she doesn't know how to defend herself."

"I don't see what that has to do with the glasses."

"It's the other children," Amanda said intently. "Every day they find evil pleasure in knocking her glasses off. Then, they try to step on them before we can pick them up. After that, she is afraid because her parents will scold her, but it's not her fault."

"Poor Laura!" Louise exclaimed.

---

7   *La Madelon*, 1913, musique Camille Robert, paroles Louis Bousquet (1870–1941). War soldier song.

"Also, she cries nearly every day."

"Maybe I could try to talk to her mother next time she comes into the shop."

"Really? Oh, Maman, that would be wonderful!"

"I said I would try because it might be difficult if someone else enters the shop at the same time."

"Especially, make sure you tell her mother it's not Laura's fault."

"I'll do my best," her mother assured her. "But right now, you need to start eating."

A hot potato slowly cooled down on Amanda's plate, next to a big piece of camembert.[8]

"Papa, every day, on the way to school, there are some bullies who are looking for a fight," Jean-Baptiste suddenly spoke up, as his sister burned the tip of her fingers, trying to peel the potato.

"Well," Armand declared severely, "I don't want to hear one of you has started a fight. As far as I'm concerned, that's forbidden."

He reached over to help his daughter.

"I've heard they're going to beat us, too," Amanda added. "Perrine told me."

"It's a custom around here," her brother explained. "They say it's because we're new. So, we have to pass some kind of a test. They call us: les étrangers!"

"They even called me a Parisienne!" Amanda confirmed.

Armand smiled.

"I suppose that, coming from farmers, it's an insult. In Paris, when a vehicle is too slow we call the driver: paysan."[9]

"But what are we to do if they start kicking us?" inquired Jean-Baptiste.

"If they touch me," Amanda declared with her mouth full, "I'll punch their face."

Their father pushed his plate away.

"You're certainly not allowed to strike anyone in the face. If

---

8 French cow cheese
9 Farmer

somebody starts a fight with you, not answering will often be enough to stop any further attempt."

"And what if it's not enough?" Amanda insisted.

"What do these kids fight for, anyway?" Louise asked.

"To reassess who is the leader—" Jean-Baptiste answered.

"Then," Amanda interrupted, "Jean-Baptiste will have to fight anyone the leader decides—maybe several at a time. If he beats them all, then he'll fight with the leader."

Jean-Baptiste glimpsed at his sister.

"They also beat up tattletales. Tattling is one of the worst offences around here: it's considered as a betrayal worthy of punishment. From what I heard, even parents avoid to get mixed up when their children settle accounts."

"They probably want to avoid getting into feuds," Louise remarked.

Armand sighed.

"Meanwhile, their children beat up newcomers to see what they're made of."

He got up.

"Alright. I'll show you one thing. It's useless to kick high up, for the other person can then grab your foot and send you rolling to the ground."

His action demonstrated his words. Amanda understood right away.

"Very well, then. If someone tries to kick me high, I'll grab their foot."

"Now, I'm going to show you how to kick low, to the shin. Come here, Jean-Baptiste."

Armand demonstrated and laughed.

He declared, "When my father was in the army, there was a corporal who knew boxing. My father had a rather handsome nose. So, this man kept provoking him to fight. My Papa suspected he wanted to mess up his nose. One day, he had enough. He fought back."

He stood in a defensive position.

"Then wham! He gave him the famous low kick to the shin. The other man bent completely over. After that, he never bothered my father again."

Jean-Baptiste and Amanda were delighted.

"Please, Papa, do it again!" his son exclaimed.

"Tell us another story like this," Amanda begged.

"That's enough for today," their father answered. "It's time to go to bed."

Then he added, "And tomorrow, I'll accompany you to school."

THE TEST

ARMAND ACCOMPANIED HIS CHILDREN TO SCHOOL every morning and afternoon. Laura, the neighbor girl, found this system very convenient. As soon as she saw the Vissac family step out of their home to go to school, she ran to join the little clan. Armand took her to his heart right away and he always welcomed her kindly.

"Good morning little rose," he often said.

Then, a wide toothless smile would spread over the face of the six-year-old child as she slid her slim hand into his big, strong one. Meanwhile, Amanda ran ahead with her new friend, Perrine, the baker's daughter.

Soon, Laura wore a new pair of glasses. Consequently, the other school children found this situation rather upsetting. No other father accompanied his children to school, and this new situation thwarted their plans. They held a war council.

"We can't do nothing anymore," André complained. "Their father is always there."

"He'll never let us fight on the street," Robert went on.

"Much less against his own kids," Yves chimed in. "This is an impossible situation."

"I don't agree. If we can't fight in the street anymore, we'll fight in the school yard," Joël suggested.

"You're crazy," Yves retorted. "There's the teacher."

"Come on! When the weather is cold, she never comes outside, and when she has a lot of work to do, she doesn't even look up to see what's going on," André answered, for he liked the idea.

"I agree," Joël approved. "We'll stand guard. We'll wait for just the right time. In any case, these foreigners must pass the test! Besides, I have an account to settle with the Parisienne."

"And in the afternoon, to go back home, we'll take a big detour around the back of the village so le Père Vissac can't catch us," André added.

Perrine heard all about their plan from her big brother. She and Laura informed Amanda as soon as they entered the school yard. Laura trembled all over.

"They're going to take you to the torture post," she warned, pointing to one of the posts in the covered playground.

"They'll hold you and beat you 'til you cry," Perrine added.

The other girls surrounded them and in their shrill voices described the tortures, each more *pleasant* than the other.

"They'll scalp you!"

Amanda shrugged.

"How come you aren't afraid?" Isabelle could not help asking, somewhat impressed.

She was André's sister. He was the leader of the band.

Amanda did not answer Isabelle. She did not mind fighting, and she was determined to defend herself. Her father had not forbidden *that*!

The bell rang. The children got in line, whispering to each other with looks of conspiracy on their faces.

* * *

During recess that day, the teacher remained inside. It was cold outside and she always had a lot of work to do—she taught first through third grades in the one classroom.

In the courtyard, the oldest boys led Jean-Baptiste away. He followed his father's instructions. First, he tried not to answer their provocations. Meanwhile, he anxiously kept an eye on his little sister; also surrounded.

Amanda could hear sneering all around her. She was in the middle of a crowd slowly closing in on her. So, she first tried to put enough space between her and the threatening torture post, but like a net, the circle closed suddenly upon her. Bravely she faced the grinning smiles—her arms crossed on her chest and her eyes threw defiant looks.

"Come and get me if you are not afraid!" she provoked.

The boys, surprised, stopped for a minute. Two of them carefully moved closer. She clenched her fists and quickly did a few circles with both arms. They backed up to avoid the blows. She then slowly started towards the post under the covered yard.

"You want to get me next to the post, right?" she mocked. "Look, it's easy. All you have to do is ask me nicely. What next? You want to play little red Indians?"

She added, "Now, if you touch me, I warn you: you'll have to deal with my father."

The argument was serious and the threat real.

"He won't catch us. We'll go home by the back way."

"Have you ever thought he's able to take the back way, too?"

The boys were disgusted.

"Come on, leave her alone," the leader declared abruptly.

"Yeah, she's not even scared," his lieutenant added. "It's not even funny!"

"Well then, let's go find the other one, instead."

The little band turned towards Jean-Baptiste. Feet flew in his direction. He backed up to avoid them. Suddenly he seized a foot, gathered all his strength, and sent a big boy rolling to the ground.

The teacher yelled, "Jean-Baptiste Vissac!"

The boys scattered quickly while Jean-Baptiste walked slowly to the schoolhouse. He saw, with relief, his little sister was safe.

"You stay in detention during recess!" the teacher ordered.

Nobody dared to discuss this wrong, but the two foreigners had won the respect of the farmer boys. From now on, they were not to be called foreigners anymore.

* * *

School was over. Amanda stepped out of the courtyard and looked up, staring into the immensity of the sky over Grande Rue. In the distance, her father was coming. Yet, she had the strange feeling someone more powerful than he was watching over her.

LAURA

THE SCHOOL TEACHER WAS THE OWNER of a long, wooden stick, which she kept under her front desk on the stage. She used it as a pointer for the black board. She also had no hesitation using it to maintain discipline.

One day, in anger, she beat François's head and shoulders so hard, and with so many blows, the stick broke in two. The children, who watched with awe, sighed with relief.

"No more stick, no more blows," they reasoned.

The next morning, after they were all seated in their places, they were greatly surprised when the teacher again waved the famous stick as she went throughout the rows of her oldest students. It had an immediate effect. The classroom filled with respectful silence.

"She went out and cut another one," Amanda whispered to Perrine.

"No, it's the same one," her seatmate answered.

"You are right, the tip looks like the other one."

"It's a magic wand!"

"No! Really?"

"I'm telling you. Look, it came back together into one piece."

"Or maybe it grew back."

The word spread in the younger children's row.

"It's a magical wand!"

When the teacher arrived next to Amanda, she gazed open-eyed and realized the legendary stick had been carefully taped back together.

She thought, *probably with a whole roll of scotch tape.*

As for the teacher, she enjoyed her regained authority.

* * *

In the afternoon, while the older children recited their history lesson, Amanda was sometimes so bored she could not find anything better to do than chat with Perrine. Unfortunately, this activity badly interfered with the older children's class.

The teacher, however, had found a solution to that problem. Every day she regularly sent one of the two girls to kneel down in the front corner of the room, each one in turn, until the lesson was over. Amanda found this situation less boring, as she busied herself, trying to keep her balance moving from one knee to the other, so it did not hurt too much.

* * *

In the morning, the teacher asked each of the first graders to come to the big desk situated in the back of the room to test his or her reading ability. Amanda's desk was right next to the big desk, across the aisle. She already knew how to read, so when her turn was over, she went back to her seat and was bored again. Then, she started whispering some exciting tales to Perrine.

One day, as she forgot to control the pitch of her voice, a stinging, abrupt slap to her face interrupted her. At the same time, she heard the stern verdict of the teacher:

"Pipelette!"[10]

---

10 Chatterbox

All heads turned. The silence in the class was so pervasive she felt her whole face turn red. She refused to cry or even touch her painful cheek.

When she got out of school, the sting of the blow was still sharp. She slowly passed her fingertips over her face and felt a distinct mark.

"Jean-Baptiste, can you see it?"

"A little bit, yes."

"You won't tell Maman, will you?"

"D'accord, if you don't tell on me, either, when she hits me."

"D'accord."

Amanda sighed deeply and slowly started on her way home. She sneaked into the house and headed for the mirror. Her teacher's handprint was right there, on her face. Then, what she feared the most happened: as soon as her mother stepped into the kitchen, she noticed it.

"Amanda, what happened to you?"

"I ran into a tree," she answered elusively.

"Amanda, if your teacher ever hits you, I want you to tell me. I'll go and talk to her."

"Oh no, please don't! If you do, she might just hate me. Besides, she's just treating me like everyone else. In any case, it's better than being hit with the stick."

"Oh!"

"It's true; she's right," Jean-Baptiste said, flying to his sister's rescue.

"She doesn't have the right to hit anyone," their mother protested.

Jean-Baptiste thought for a second.

"Maybe in Thym she does. Everyone here believes it's the only way to get some schooling into the heads of the farmer kids."

"Yeah, no one ever complains about it," Amanda concluded.

Graciously, Louise did not insist. She later found out while talking with her customers, the actual law—which no one fully understood—did not matter much in the way discipline was kept in the primary school of Thym.

* * *

The teacher scared Laura. In her presence, she would go into such a panic when she was asked to read. She could barely utter a single word and if she tried a syllable, it was never the right one.

The day came when Laura started to cry even before she got to the reading desk. Thick tears blurred her glasses. The impatient teacher slapped her on the face and sent her right back to her seat.

"You're hopeless. You'll never read."

The poor glasses flew to the ground. Amanda got up to get them. It just happened that Perrine was not there that day. She was sick with German measles and her seat was empty. Amanda made a sign to Laura to sit next to her. The distressed child, still shocked, obeyed like a robot.

This couldn't possibly get worse.

Amanda wiped the glasses on her school blouse and waited patiently until her little friend dried her tears.

Then, she whispered to her, "Do you know there's nothing easier than learning to read?"

The wild idea she could teach someone to read had just dawned on her. Laura sadly shook her head.

"I'll never be able to do that."

"Don't be silly; listen to me. We'll start at the beginning. Look at this letter: this is an A."

"I'll never remember that."

"Yes you will. It's easy. Just think of the *As*. It's the same sound and it's the strongest card in a deck of cards. The next letter is B. Just think of *Bébé!*"

Laura got carried away with the game. Amanda, very excited, started to talk louder. Then, with a protecting motion, she quickly turned toward the teacher. She realized the lady had been observing them. The teacher simply frowned.

* * *

The next day, when it was Laura's turn to read, the teacher told Amanda, "Take care of her, will you? Maybe you'll get something out of her."

The fact the hard disciplinarian teacher entrusted Amanda with a student filled the girl with pride.

When Perrine returned to school, after her illness was over, and took her seat, the teacher decided it was time for her to take back her illiterate student. When she called for Laura to come up to the reading desk, the child grew pale and her knees began to shake.

"You can do it," Amanda whispered to encourage her as she passed.

Laura took her place by the teacher and read her first words. She had won the battle.

THE CRAYONS

ARMAND HAD ACQUIRED A GREEN VAN with the inside covered with shelves. Once every two days, he drove to the countryside to sell groceries while Louise kept the shop. During vacation, he sometimes took Jean-Baptiste or Amanda along. Thus, the children discovered where most of their schoolmates lived.

They flew by on narrow roads, which allowed only one vehicle to pass at a time. Sometimes, grass grew in the middle of the poorly tarred way.

One day, as they stopped at Evelyne's farm, Amanda saw her many brothers working hard with pitchforks. Evelyne, dressed in a big apron, appeared on the doorstep to greet her, shyly. Her sisters remained hidden in the kitchen. From that day on, Amanda stopped wondering why these young farmers never knew their lessons.

Further away, as they approached another farm, she exclaimed, "Phew! It smells awful here."

"It's the Vertreks' farm. They make sour corn to feed their cows."

"Well then, I now understand why François and his sister smell so bad. It's a shame, for they are good children, but everybody stays away from them. Even the teacher put them at the back of the classroom, for this reason. One day, she broke her stick on François' head because he never learns his lessons. Even I don't like to come

close to them. I think because of this, they don't try very hard to
learn. Say, is it still far?" she asked while plugging her nose.

"Ah! It smells about two kilometers around. It's disgusting and
it's a shame for their children. I'm going to talk to that little lady!"

A good woman came out to meet the van to buy her groceries.
Armand served her, courteously.

Once she had paid he said, "Say, it stinks here with your corn.
Couldn't you feed your cows something different?"

The lady stared at him with eyes round with surprise.

"We don't smell anything."

"You must have gotten used to it. Think of your children, when
they go to school. They smell bad and everybody stays away from
them."

"The children? They're not very gifted at studying, anyway."

"All the more! It can't be much fun for them to be systematically
sent to the back of the class, or left out. You should talk to your
husband. If I ever see him, I'll tell him."

The woman shrugged, wondering if he was serious. When they
hit the road again, Amanda was proud of her father. He did not
hesitate to say things, but he was so kind none of his customers ever
held a grudge against him.

* * *

Amanda had been so bored in the first grade; when she got into
the second, she happily chose her new seat on the front row. Even
though François was cleanly dressed, he was still sent to the back of
the room.

One morning, before she entered the classroom, Isabelle was
very excited.

"My godmother came to see me yesterday!"

She spoke loudly, and the girls gathered around her.

"She gave me a present . . . look at it! I brought it with me!"

She bent down, opened her school bag, and proudly pulled out a box of pastels. The girls shouted with surprise. The soft colors were simply beautiful.

Amanda's eyes shined with envy. She had never seen anything so lovely! Isabelle put the precious crayons back into her bag.

During recess, each student left his or her school bag next to his or her desk. Isabelle's desk was two rows behind Amanda's on the same aisle. The entry door was in the back of the classroom. To go out, Amanda had to pass by Isabelle's desk.

That day, as the morning break started, Amanda managed to be the last one in the room. She glanced toward the teacher, who looked down at a lesson, and then moved forward, like a cat, and discreetly stooped down, plunging her hand into Isabelle's bag.

It was a simple one-pocket bag, and nearly empty. This surprised her. She saw the crayons, right away, and seized them, sliding them under her sweater. The whole operation had lasted no longer than that of a genuflection. She continued outside, as peacefully as possible.

"Amanda, come and play!"

"No, thank you. I don't feel like playing today."

Her hand lightly rested on her stomach. Perrine observed her so closely she felt embarrassed. Usually she never refused to run.

"Are you sick?"

"Non. Well . . . maybe. I don't know."

After recess was over, she managed to be the first one in the classroom. She let the product of her theft slide down between the books of her schoolbag. She felt better.

* * *

At the end of the day, Amanda was lightheartedly putting her school materials back into her bag when a shrilling scream of distress resounded behind her.

"My godmother's crayons . . . they're not here anymore . . . teacher! Somebody has stolen my crayons!"

Isabelle burst into tears. The teacher took pity on her. She reacted rapidly.

"Immediately call back those who are already outside!"

Two or three pupils rushed outside to execute the order. A group of perplexed children came back and entered the room.

"There has been a theft in the classroom," the teacher announced solemnly. "We're going to search bags."

For an unknown reason, she then slightly changed her mind. "Well, we're going to search some bags."

The children looked at each other with dismay. Isabelle sobbed abundantly. Amanda felt nervous. She hid behind her schoolmates. The teacher looked severely at her class and tried a last call.

"Has someone taken Isabelle's crayons? Let that person admit it!"

While all the honest faces were turned toward the lady, a vision arose in Amanda's mind. She saw a picture of loathing and rejection from all her school friends, forever. She put on her best innocent look and tried to remain invisible.

Suddenly, the teacher pointed to a boy, "You! Open your bag!"

He obeyed, humiliated. His bag was empty. Another boy went through the same treatment, but in vain. The piercing eyes of the teacher slid on the faces, scrutinizing them, one after another. They passed above Amanda's head and rested on Laura. The poor child lost her self-control; her face went through shades of color, and she started to tremble.

"Open your bag!" the teacher ordered.

Laura was nearly crying. Amanda could not help wondering why. She had nothing to fear. The teacher, soon discouraged, gave up the search and uttered a last word of advice.

"Don't bring anything precious into school."

A few girls surrounded Isabelle, but she would not be comforted. The others spread out quietly. Amanda imitated them, her honor safe.

* * *

Once at home, she opened her bag and pulled out her stolen treasure. She started to color. Shortly afterwards, her mother saw the pretty crayons.

"Where did you get these?"

"Isabelle gave them to me."

"This is really kind of her. When I see her mother, I'll thank her."

At the grocery store, Louise knew everybody.

"No, there's no need for that. Actually, she just loaned them to me. I'm going to give them back to her."

The crayons were fragile. Soon, they were reduced to bits and pieces. It was time to get rid of this obvious testimony. Amanda threw them into the trash.

* * *

The village priest had come to the Vissac home to enroll the children in catechism. After discussing the question with her husband, Louise decided to sign them in.

"Better to have some kind of religious education than none at all," she determined.

"The best religious education is through modeling," Armand answered.

"Both are useful."

"Of course, but what I mean is all the parents send their children to catechism, but there's not one who goes to mass. Well, as far as I'm concerned, I'll go along with my children!"

Then he started to sing:

> "I know of a church at the far end of a hamlet
> Whose fine steeple reflects in the water,
> In the pure water of a river,

And often, tired at the fall of the night,
I come here, slowly,
Far from the noise of the city,
To say a prayer."[11]

Armand kept his word. Most of the time, he was the only man to show up in church apart from the priest. Soon, he became known as a religious man and all the other women from the village became envious of Louise.

However, Armand never went to confession, nor took communion. He also did not pray to either the virgin, or the saints.

He said, "It's better to address the Good Lord than his saints."

* * *

Once a year, the children of the parish, who were enrolled to study the catechism, had to go to confession. For Amanda, it was the first time. A catechism lady prepared them, but the priest would receive their confessions.

The lady had them sit in an empty room with wide spaces between them. They were to concentrate their whole memories, and write their sins on square pieces of white paper in full secrecy.

Amanda could not help glancing toward a few bullies. They surely had fascinating stories to tell. Unfortunately, once someone had gone to confession, he would leave directly from there and go back home.

The priest called, "Yves!"

Not even a minute had passed when he came back with the boy.

"I can't have you come with an empty paper," he said. "Sit down and try again."

---

11 La Petite Eglise, 1896 poésie Charles Fallot (1874–1939), 1902 musique Paul Delmet (1862–1904).

This priest did not seem to be too credulous. He decided to turn to the girls. Amanda was very thankful for the important story she had to tell. She lifted her hand to go in right away. He made a sign for her to come.

She followed him into the dark and empty church to the sculpted-wood confessional, which had two doors, side-by-side. She entered through one and sat down as the religious man took his place in the next-door closet. A lattice window separated them from each other; she was surprised to barely see his face.

He started to recite the usual introduction, and then stopped. It was her turn. With some hesitation, she went down her list.

"I envied my school friend for her crayons. I stole them. I lied to hide them. I hurt her feelings, badly because she cried a lot for her loss. Finally, I broke those crayons, and I threw them into the trash. I'm asking for forgiveness and have decided I'll never steal again."

With a neutral tone, the priest declaimed, "Je t'absous au nom du Père, du Fils et du Saint-Esprit.[12] Go in peace."

He was satisfied, but Amanda felt as guilty as before.

What to do?

The priest was supposed to forget the whole thing. Year after year, with a few changes here or there, just in case he remembered, she could reuse the same story. At least the ugly incident would become useful for something.

---

12 I absolve you in the name of the Father, Son, and Holy Spirit

THE ISLAND OF NOIRMOUTIER

AT THE BEGINNING OF THE SUMMER 1969, the Vissac family moved again, but this time they did not go any further than the edge of the village, farthest away from the primary school. Armand had found a job as a mechanic-driver at the agricultural garage of the village.

The Thymerais took pride in being part of what was commonly called "The Silo of France."[13] Eventually, Louise also found a job as an accountant-secretary in another agricultural garage in the area.

Armand decided to wait until the end of the summer school vacation to sell his green van. He had the great idea of using it for transportation to go on vacation to the sea. He removed the shelves. With a bench set across the length of the van, they would be able to travel with the grandparents and the so-sweet Tante Mimi who had joined them from Belfort.

Oncle Jacques, Tante Irène, and the cousins had already arrived on the island of Noirmoutier where they had rented a bungalow. They waited for them.

On the big day of the departure, everybody was joyful. Louise made sure they all knew the law.

"It's forbidden to travel in the back of a van on a bench."

---

13 "Le Grenier de la France"

Pépère took his place on the passenger seat on the front and fiercely watched for any blue French military cap that would show up. Then, he sounded the alarm.

"Everyone to the floor!"

The children tumbled down from the bench while the women bent over—half from laughter, half from fright. Nevertheless, they arrived without any problem at the city of Le Mans.

"Well!" Mémère exclaimed, "I declare; we must not just pass by here without buying at least one jar of the famous rillettes of Le Mans."

Her proposal was welcomed with enthusiasm, for it was getting close to lunchtime. Therefore, they bought the rillettes and Armand started to look for a picnic place. He finally came to a pretty, country trail where he stopped the van.

Tante Mimi hurried to spread a tablecloth on the grass, which would be the table. Amanda religiously carried the big jar of ham pâté and sat it in the middle of the empty tablecloth.

While her grandmother and mother were in the van preparing the rest of the meal, she sat in front of the tablecloth and Pépère came to keep her company. He sat across from her; the jar of rillettes exactly in between the two of them.

Suddenly, he looked up to the sky.

"Oh ! On dirait qu'on sent des gouttes. . ."[14] he noticed.

Amanda, her eyes fixed on the jar, answered slowly.

"Oh non, moi je ne m'en dégoute pas!"[15]

Pépère stared back at her, puzzled for a minute. Behind them, a roll of laughter shook the vehicle. Slightly surprised, Amanda saw everybody come out of it one-by-one.

Mémère held her sides with laughter, her mother wiped her eyes, and Tante Mimi prudently sat on the step, dangerously shaken with a pile of plates in her hands. Her father and Jean-Baptiste

---

14 "It feels like rain drops." It could also mean: "It looks like we are tired of it."

15 "No, I am not tired of it!"

joined in. Only Amanda was not laughing.

"You just did a fine play on words with Pépère!" her mother finally explained when she could speak again.

Amanda smiled sheepishly and said, "I thought you were making fun of me being greedy."

* * *

That afternoon, the trip seemed longer. Occasionally, Pépère exchanged his comfortable seat with Mémère's. During one of his visits at the back of the van, he put on his best professorial expression and addressed his grandchildren.

"It's important that we arrive tonight before the tide or it won't be possible to drive to the island on dry land anymore. Do you know the ocean moves forward at the speed of a running horse, and it covers the road all the way to the island?"

After he had regained his place at the front, Amanda could not help meditating on what would happen if the van broke down during the crossing. Therefore, when they finally arrived at the terminus of their trip, with a mixed feeling of excitement and fear—standing between her father and her grandfather—she saw their vehicle engage on this Red Sea passage that would soon be covered by the waters.

Thank goodness, the crossing didn't take long.

* * *

On the other side, out on the island, Oncle Jacques, Tante Irène, and the cousins impatiently waited for them. The two youngest had lost their blond locks and they now looked like real little boys. Jean-Baptiste was slightly younger than Mélissa. He loved his cousin.

In spite of three, very active brothers, she never departed from her gentleness that reflected in her wide, brown eyes. Romain, the oldest, looked bold. Amanda admired him; he was so handsome with his limpid blue eyes in a face already tanned by the sunshine.

"Come on," Oncle Jacques said. "I'm going to show you the way to your bungalow. You must get settled before nightfall."

"Not already!" Amanda protested.

"What do you mean not already? Tomorrow you'll have plenty of time to play all day long."

Romain turned to her.

"Tomorrow I'll come and wake you up at sunrise," he teased her.

"Oui, s'il te plaît!"

"Well, then, after I've gone shrimp hunting!" he promised, this time seriously.

That night, Amanda fell asleep, thinking of her cousin's promise.

* * *

The next morning, when Romain arrived, the sun was already high up in the sky, but Jean-Baptiste and Amanda had not yet finished their breakfast. Their cousin held up a little bucket, half-filled with water.

"Look at all I've caught!" he said proudly. "I have found a great place."

"Ho!" their grandfather exclaimed. "I love shrimp!"

"Here, Pépère!" Romain offered generously. "It's for you."

Pépère did not wait any longer. In front of the curious eyes of his three grandchildren, he rinsed the little animals, dumped them into a pot, filled it with boiling water, and added this light supplement to his own breakfast. Then, he drew a deep sigh.

"It was just enough for one person."

"If we put our efforts together, we could bring back much more than that," Jean-Baptiste suggested.

"Oui!" Amanda shouted. "This is a great idea. Romain, can we go back to get some more?"

"Not today," he answered.

"Why not?"

She was disappointed.

"We must go very early in the morning," her cousin explained kindly, "before the tide comes in. This is the reason why I just arrived. Now, it's too late to go shrimp hunting, but it's a good time to go swimming."

"Well then, when *can* we go shrimp hunting?"

"Tomorrow morning," Oncle Jacques answered.

"Can we really go tomorrow morning?"

"However, I won't be able to accompany you," he remarked.

He hesitated, but the children looked at him so intently he finally made a proposal.

"I think Romain is perfectly able to accompany you, along with Mélissa. However, first, I must ask your Tante, and you'll have to get up at sunrise."

"I'll come and get you early, and I'll show you my place," Romain offered right away.

Amanda danced for joy.

"This is wonderful! Meanwhile, let's go to the shore."

The day went by very fast—bathing, exploring, and playing. It was great to be together again.

SHRIMP HUNTING

AFTER A GOOD NIGHT'S SLEEP, THE children got up, fresh and ready to go. Their grandparents were still in bed when Romain and Mélissa finally arrived. They were loaded with buckets and scoopnets: there was a bucket and a net for each one of them.

Once fully equipped, they set off, impatient to hunt enough shrimp to feed the whole family. The sun was already high in the sky. They followed Romain, the undisputed expedition leader.

Amanda wondered how he could find his way so easily. To her, it all looked the same. She was unable to recognize the shore where they had bathed the previous day. Instead of the playful waves, there remained only a few scattered puddles where shrimp thrived.

Romain, however, did not allow them to stop.

"Let's hurry before the tide comes in!"

He guided them even further away, at a quick pace, in a landscape of wet sand and viscous seaweed that smelled like iodine. Amanda felt a little nervous. She had the impression her legs were too short; they were not moving fast enough. Mélissa patiently waited for her, as if her protector.

"Romain, slow down, will you! Amanda is the youngest of us here," she reminded her brother.

The boy turned around and looked at his younger cousin. He encouraged her briefly and tried to slow down.

"Are you okay? We're nearly there."

He pointed his finger toward a rocky mass that emerged from the sand. As they kept getting closer, the mass grew bigger. When they arrived at the foot of the place, it was taller than Romain and about as large as a living room.

With their clasped hands, the boys made a step, each one for his girl cousin. Then, they climbed after them, clenching on the rough surface of the rock. They pulled themselves up to the top and disappeared on the inside of the site.

Once there, they discovered the rocks were entirely encompassing a little natural beach made of fine sand. It was hidden from any outsiders and covered with water that barely came up to their ankles.

"Look!" Jean-Baptiste exclaimed. "It's full of shrimp."

"Yes," Mélissa explained. "Just feel how soft the sand is here, and the water is still warm! The shrimp love this place."

The children set themselves to work right away. Jean-Baptiste and Mélissa decided to pull their efforts together to fill a bucket faster. Just as they had put down their half-filled bucket in the warm water, Amanda—eyes fixed on her net—backed up and bumped into it.

The bucket fell over, freeing all of its little prisoners. Jean-Baptiste was upset, but Mélissa did not lose her cheerfulness so easily.

"Don't worry, we'll have it full again in no time."

"I'll help you," Amanda offered.

This time, the bucket was nearly full when Jean-Baptiste knocked it over. The children became discouraged. Only Romain's bucket remained intact.

Suddenly, Amanda, who was the smallest, remarked, "It's becoming harder to see the bottom of the sea. It seems like the water is rising. It's coming up to my calves."

Romain looked up immediately. Without a word, he climbed like a cat to the top of the rocks.

He shouted, "The tide! We're surrounded!"

He rapidly made it back to the bottom.

"Is it bad?" Amanda asked anxiously.

"We must get out of here as fast as possible," he answered simply. "Come on, let's climb back up."

The boys helped their cousins again, giving them a starting lift from their hands that were crossed together. When they reached the top of the rocks, they discovered a watery mass at their feet surrounding them on every side. Far away, they could spot the shore.

Mélissa took a quick survey of the situation. With her usual calm, she drew an emergency plan.

"Jean-Baptiste and I can swim. We'll go first and try to reach the shore. May God give us the necessary strength. If everything is alright, we'll wave to you to try to join us."

"But I can't swim," Amanda said with a little voice, "and I can't touch the bottom here."

"Don't worry, cousin. I'll swim for two. You'll climb on my back," Romain offered.

He had adopted his sister's plan without arguing.

"If there should be any problem, we'll already be at a place to call for help, immediately. Meanwhile, we'll pray for you," she added.

Without any more delay, she and Jean-Baptiste jumped into the water.

Noticing the nervous look on her cousin's face, Mélissa shouted to her, "Don't worry! My brother is strong!"

As Amanda kept staring at the two heads moving slowly, but surely away, Romain plunged down to test the depth of the water.

When he reappeared, he asked: "Can you see them?"

"Yeah, they're alright."

At last, Mélissa and Jean-Baptiste waved vigorously from the shore.

"It's our turn," Amanda declared.

"Are you afraid?" Romain inquired.

"I'm okay."

"Alright, now listen to me. You're going to get on my back and hold me at the shoulders. For goodness sake, don't grab my neck."

Amanda had never jumped into the water with her clothes on. Neither had her life depended on such a young, however excellent, swimmer. She hesitated.

"Have you ever done that before?"

The bright blue eyes twinkled in the morning sun.

"Don't forget I have two little brothers."

"Maybe, but I've never done that before."

Romain was happy Amanda had not panicked.

"Come on," he encouraged gently. "There's no way I can leave you here."

She obeyed, letting herself slide slowly onto his back. She grabbed him at the shoulders. He firmly held onto the rock, which was now about entirely covered by the sea.

He measured her weight, and then shouted, "Watch out, we'll dive!"

Before Amanda could close her mouth tight, the two children disappeared under the water. She felt his firm muscles cut through the mass and tried to not hinder their movements. It seemed like she had been in this underworld for an eternity, and she was going to choke forever when Romain came to the surface long enough for them to catch their breath. Then he plunged again, but this time was not as long.

He felt the ground under his feet and stood up—his head: barely above the water; his rider: suffocating and spitting salty water onto his back.

"I can touch the ground," he announced. "We're alright, but stay on my back; it's still too deep for you."

He walked a few more meters, and then he decided,

"Get down. I think you can walk now."

The girl regretted having to leave such a secure place, but she could touch the ground. With her head barely above the water, she staggered. He grabbed her hand, and they walked a few more steps.

Once it looked like it was safe for her, he released his grip. They looked at each other with relief.

"You're okay?" he asked, amused by the half-asphyxiated face of his cousin.

"You made me drink some salty water!" she reproached.

"And you are heavy," he retorted.

She knew she had hurt his feelings. She tried to look him in the eyes, but could not help blinking.

Was it the light reflecting on the water that was too bright, or his piercing glance?

"Well . . . you saved my life. Thank you!" she said sincerely.

He turned around before she could add anything else.

"I'm going to try to get the rest of our fishing tools. I'll let you join Mélissa and Jean-Baptiste by yourself. You'll be alright, won't you?"

"Yes, I will."

She sighed. She hated to see him go back.

* * *

Mélissa welcomed her warmly.

"*Merci Seigneur!* Everything is alright. We prayed for you the whole time you were under the water."

Amanda stared at her with curiosity.

* * *

As soon as Romain returned, the children started on their way home. The heat of the sun combined with the ocean breeze to dry their clothes quickly. They hurried, concerned their parents would worry, but Pépère waited for them with a greedy look on his face. When he realized he had to be thankful for the same amount of shrimp as the day before, he declared they were simply tastier than ever.

It could be Mélissa gave an account of their adventure to Tante Irène, for from this day on, Mémère declared if they wanted to eat shrimp, they would have to go buy them at the marketplace.

* * *

Jean-Baptiste and Amanda always spent wonderful vacations with their cousins. This would be the only summer they would have such a family gathering at the sea.

However, as soon as she had an opportunity, Louise took her little family to Alsace, her childhood region. There, visiting the cousins, the children spent memorable hours constructing dams in the icy water of a mountain brook, trying to ride a pig on the woody slopes of the Vosges, and baking potatoes under the ashes of a wood fire.

THE NEW GIRL

AMANDA WAS TEN YEARS OLD WHEN she entered her last year of primary school. To break the monotony of the school routine, Louise enrolled her in a music class. She wanted to play the violin, very much. As for her mother, she wished Amanda would play the piano.

It just happened the town of La Serpe, where the music school was located, had taken on a new violin teacher. While the piano classes were filled to the brim, the director still had very few students for the violin class. Therefore, he sought to recruit students for the string instrument, which established Amanda's happiness. Besides, the music school loaned out the violin.

One evening, as she played on her instrument, an elderly neighbor lady knocked at their door. Louise opened it. Her daughter, curious, interrupted her music to join her.

"Good evening, Madame Vissac."

"Good evening, Madame Riviera."

The old lady looked embarrassed.

"Excuse me, but I came to ask you for a little favor. My children work in the city and they just built a new house on the outskirts of the village. The house isn't finished yet, but my granddaughter has come to live with me until they can move in. She is a little bit shy, and I was wondering if your daughter could stop at my home to pick her up and accompany her to school tomorrow morning. It would be just on her way."

"Yes, I will, Madame Riviera, with pleasure!" Amanda accepted right away.

The grandmother gave her a thankful smile.

"I trust you, Amanda. I know you're a good girl. You two are the same age. Maybe you could introduce her to the others."

"Don't worry; I'll take care of her," she promised.

* * *

The next morning, Amanda got up early. Her new mission excited her. When she arrived at Madame Riviera's, a girl her age was waiting for her. Long, curly, blond hair framed her delicate face, making her blue eyes seem wider.

"Salut! Are you ready?"

The old lady kissed her granddaughter good-bye, and with slight anxiety, watched her walk away. The girl had not spoken yet.

"My name is Amanda. What's your name?"

"Linda."

"Would you like us to be friends?"

Linda was hesitant. Amanda waited for an answer.

"If you want to."

"Of course, I want to. Don't worry; I'm going to introduce you to the others. They aren't real bad."

She giggled and added, "You look like a fairy. You'll be the prettiest of us all."

The girl blushed with the compliment.

Amanda went on, "You'll see. Le maître, Monsieur Simon, is really good. He never shouts and never hits. Even the worst bully respects him. Only, sometimes . . ."

Linda stopped in her tracks and held her breath. Her new friend bit her lip and finished.

". . . sometimes he looks like he is a little sad. Well, you'll see. In any case, I think he's great. Here's the school. We've arrived."

★ ★ ★

The schoolroom for the fourth and fifth graders stood at the center of the village in the shadow of the church steeple. The two girls had barely stepped into the courtyard when the other children ran to them from all directions, surrounding them.

"A new girl!"

"Who's she?"

"This is Linda, a new friend. She's nice and you'd better be nice to her, too," Amanda answered.

"Wait a minute! You're not going to dictate our lives now," André threw in. "You know very well that strangers here have to take a test."

"She's not a stranger. Her grandmother is from this village."

"So what? She's new. We're going to beat her first, and then we can discuss it," Joël insisted.

Amanda sighed and glanced at the newcomer. The lass had turned pale. She stepped in front of Linda.

"No way. It's rather stupid, and if you're going to touch her, you'll have to fight with me first."

The boys closed on her.

"You're a party spoiler."

Amanda searched with her eyes for Valérie Ruelle, the daughter of rich farmers and respected by her schoolmates, but for now she kept at a distance from the crowd and observed the scene from far away.

"Valérie!" Amanda called, hoping to get her support. "Come here!"

The girl walked slowly toward them, obviously without any enthusiasm. She dragged alongside her two of her friends.

When she got close enough, she asked, "What do you want?"

"Don't tell me you agree with them!" Amanda exclaimed.

Valérie shrugged. "Of course, not!"

"It's settled then," Amanda concluded quickly. "You boys leave her alone."

"Why do you have to always side with her?" Joël shouted to Valérie.

"Because her Maman teaches catechism," Colette sang.

Valérie pinched her lips. As the children disbanded, André passed by Amanda.

"We lost a great opportunity forever," he grumbled.

She shrugged. Valérie and a few other girls gathered around Linda.

"My name is Perrine."

"I'm Cécile."

"I'm Aurélie, and we all go to catechism. My mother teaches catechism, too."

"Well, if you're nice to me, I'll show you one of the city games," Linda offered right away.

When M. Simon stepped outside to call his students to class, he saw, with pleasure, the newcomer led the whole class in a game.

* * *

Valérie integrated Linda into her circle of friends. One morning, not long after her arrival, she assembled her playmates. Amanda joined the group.

"You, go away!" Valérie told her bluntly. "Why do you always have to stick to me?"

"I don't stick to you any more than anybody else," she answered.

"We don't need you," Valérie insisted.

Amanda sighed. She would live through it. She went away.

"Alright, I'm leaving."

Valérie slid her arms under the arms of two of her followers and pursued her.

"I never want to play with you again," she shouted.

Amanda shrugged and turned around.

"You don't have to."

"You'll see. Two days from now, you'll come and beg us to take you back, but it's finished; you hear me? Finished for good."

"Alright. Just what did I do to you?"

"What you did? Are you stupid? You know very well what you did!"

Amanda shook her head.

"You could at least tell me—"

"You think you're the best because you rank first in the class, but you forget I rank first, too. You're too proud!"

Amanda opened her mouth, but no sound came out of it. Linda got closer. She glanced at her sadly and seemed to hesitate. Valérie noticed it.

"We don't like proud people, do we, girls?"

Her friends shook their heads with grunts of agreement. She turned towards Linda.

"You," she added, "if you go with her, nobody will talk to you anymore."

She turned her heels and walked away, dragging the other girls beside her. Slowly, Linda followed them, watching the ground. Amanda hoped she would turn around, but she found herself left all alone.

When it was time to go back to class, she passed by the school library and stopped. She smiled, relieved, chose a book, and went up to the teacher's desk to have it registered.

LE MAÎTRE

FIFTH GRADE SEEMED TOO EASY TO Amanda. She often finished her lesson a good while before the others were done. Her desk had a large cavity for books under the desktop, so she stuck the book she had just borrowed from the library there. As soon as she had finished her arithmetic work, she would discretely pull the book out and read a few pages.

The maître noticed her behavior and sent her several times in a row to the blackboard. Yet, her answers were always correct. The other children needed more time and made more mistakes. During break time, she managed to remain in the classroom and immersed herself in the adventures of *The Famous Five* she was reading.

After the break, the maître had all his pupils write down a dictated paragraph. Then, he wrote it on the board for them to check their spelling. Amanda had made few mistakes. Later, as M. Simon walked past her desk to check on the corrections, she hastily pushed her book back into the receptacle. He stopped and happened to notice she had misspelled the word: rythme[16]. She had forgotten the letter *h*.

"Well," he said, "for a musician, this is not very good! Take two demerits for this word and write it down a hundred times."

Valérie turned around with an ironic smile; other students

---

16 Rythme (pronounced rytm): proper French spelling for rhythm.

sneered. Amanda blushed with humiliation. The maître went straight back to his desk. She had to write the word one hundred times before she could again pull her book from its hiding place.

* * *

During the two-hour noon break, as soon as M. Simon unlocked the classroom door after lunchtime, Amanda managed to sneak inside to read in peace while the maître stayed outside. He did not seem to have noticed her.

At the end of the afternoon, she exchanged her book for another.

* * *

The next day, as soon as the classroom was opened, she stopped again in front of the library. There were still several titles of *The Famous Five* and *Mysteries*[17] she had not yet read.

The schoolchildren were already at their places when she came up to the desk of the maître to return her last borrowed book and get a new one. He was jotting something down and made her wait. Finally, he looked up.

"Non Amanda!" he said, "I can't agree to that."

She stared at him, puzzled. Behind her, the whole class became silent. As she was not moving, he explained.

"This is the third book you've taken since yesterday morning. What's wrong with you? I can't permit you to exchange books like this after reading only about half of them. Finish the one you have first."

"But, Monsieur!" she protested. "I've finished them all."

He looked her straight in the eyes.

"I don't believe you! Leave this book here and go sit down."

The girl was glued to her place.

---

17 Books written by Enid Blyton

"S'il vous plaît, Monsieur," she begged. "This is a continuation of the previous book."

"Go sit down!" he repeated firmly.

She swallowed hard, but obeyed.

"Come on!" M. Simon ordered. "Get to work, everybody!" The math drills were boring.

The maître observed Amanda. He got up and started his usual checkup, and walked slowly along the aisles. He stopped by the desk of the young bookworm. She kept writing rapidly. She was nearly done.

"Amanda!"

She stopped and looked at him.

"You're telling me you have read all these books?"

"Oui, Monsieur."

"Well, if you agree, I'm going to check on that."

All the children looked up; all the heads turned in their direction.

"I want you to write a report for tomorrow of the last book you read."

Groans of delight and approbation were heard.

"She's punished."

The teacher changed his mind.

"Rather, write it now, instead of the spelling drills."

Amanda's face brightened.

"Oh oui, Monsieur!"

He smiled. She started her new assignment right away. She wrote feverishly until break time. As the other children rushed outside for recess, she was still writing.

The maître came up to her and glanced over her shoulder. She had filled two pages. Gently, he pulled the paper from under her pen. She looked up.

"Come on," he said. "Go play."

"May I take one other book?"

"Yes, you may."

She hesitated.

"Maître, s'il vous plaît, may I stay in the classroom to read?"

"Why do you want to stay in here? There's sunshine outside."

She looked down.

"I'm bored outside."

"Play with the others!"

"They don't want me."

"What did you do to them?"

She looked at him honestly.

"Nothing, Monsieur."

He kept silent for a few seconds.

"Why don't they want to play with you then?"

She shrugged.

"I don't know."

M. Simon wavered.

"Non, Amanda," he finally answered. "It's been two days since you last went out for break. You need to get some fresh air."

"D'accord, Monsieur."

He watched the child go as she left the room, dragging her feet. As she was about to step out the door, he called her back.

"Amanda!"

She turned around.

"Could you and your mother come see me at the town hall tonight?"

"Well . . . Oui Monsieur, I suppose."

"Good, I'll have something for you."

"Alright . . . Sure."

★ ★ ★

At four o'clock, Amanda ran back home. As soon as her mother stepped in from work, she grabbed her.

"Maman! Maman! The maître wants to see us tonight. He's waiting for us at the town hall."

"Yes, I know. He still works there after school is over. What does he want?"

"I don't know, Maman. He said he would have something for me."

"Well then, let's go!"

Mother and daughter hurried to the town hall that was just next to the school. The door to M. Simon's office was open. As soon as he saw them, he got up. He had been waiting for them.

"Come in, Madame Vissac. I'm glad you came," he added, looking at his little student. "Please, sit down!"

Curious, they obeyed.

"You know, Madame Vissac, your daughter isn't like the others."

Louise turned pink with the compliment. He stopped for a second, but she would not interrupt him. He started again.

"I and your family have something in common. You might be surprised, as it's rather uncommon around here, but I love classical music. I know your girl plays the violin. Now, I have very special records, and I want to lend them to her."

Amanda's face looked dismayed.

"Oh, Monsieur, I'd be too afraid to do any damage to them."

He smiled.

"Non Amanda, I trust you and I want you to listen to them."

The face of the child relaxed.

After a brief hesitation he added, "It would be better not to talk about this, lest there be some jealousy."

M. Simon and Amanda looked at each other. They knew what he was talking about.

Louise reassured him, "Don't worry, Monsieur Simon. This won't go any further than our family."

The maître watched them leave his office, their arms loaded with his records. He looked happy.

* * *

Amanda finished primary school with the Excellence Award, equal with Valérie.[18]

---

18   5th Grade concludes French Primary School. Middle School covers 6th–9th grades.

THE HORSE RIDER

IT WAS SUMMER VACATION. AMANDA LOVED to ride her bicycle down the country trails cutting across the fields. She always came back from her outings with rosy cheeks.

One day, as she approached one of the entries to the village, she braked sharply. She had just passed a mansion situated at the end of a meadow. She had never noticed this place before. It had always been closed and empty.

Today, however, was different. A horse and its rider had just passed by the fence at a high speed. She dropped her bike on the grassy slope and climbed on the gate. Two other horses stood at one end of the meadow.

On the other side, by the house, two girls held a harnessed horse by its reins. The rider raced around the meadow and headed back her way. It was a boy. She noticed his horse had no saddle.

As he was about to pass by Amanda for the third time, the horse slowed down and came to a halt, right in front of her. Its rider appeared to be only a little older than her. His dark hair and eyes cast fiery reflections in the evening sunset.

He looked like a young page right out of a book. She stared at him, her eyes wide-open.

"Do you like horses?" he asked, without any other

introduction.

"Yes, I do."

He jumped to the ground.

"You want to come in?"

She was hesitant.

"I wouldn't want to bother you."

"You don't bother me at all. I'll introduce you to my sister and cousin." Amanda climbed over the wooden gate while the boy skillfully took off the horse's harness. He gave a wild shout that made Amanda jump as the freed horse started to gallop toward his mates at the far end of the field.

"Are you new here?" she asked.

"Yes, we're on vacation at my cousin's. I don't know anybody in this village."

As they talked, they came upon the two girls who looked at them with curiosity. The youngest looked a lot like the boy. The other girl was rather blond and pale, which made her seem like she had a more gentle nature than her cousins.

"Here's a friend," he declared. "She loves horses."

"Really?"

"Yes, I do."

"What's your name?"

"Amanda."

"I'm Julie; I'm his sister."

"I'm Sylvan, and this is my cousin, Claire."

"Have you ever ridden a horse?" Claire asked.

"Never!"

"And you wouldn't be afraid?"

"Of course, not!"

"Well, I'm scared," Claire admitted. "This is my horse, Star, but I'm afraid to ride him."

Sylvan started to laugh.

"They're scaredy-cats. Would you like to ride?"

"I'd love to."

"Claire, your horse is all fixed up to go. Would you let her ride it?"

"Sure, but I want to make sure she's not afraid!"

"Come on, climb!"

The animal was so tall Amanda could not get her foot near the stirrup. She looked so disappointed the boy smiled.

"Just wait. Claire, hold the rein!" he ordered.

His cousin obeyed. He came close to the side of the horse, turned his back against it, and crossed his hands together.

"Step on my hands!" he offered.

Thus, she managed to get onto the back of the animal. Her eyes shone with delight.

"Before I let you go, you must warm up with a few exercises," Claire declared.

Very seriously, like a ranch teacher, she ordered Amanda to sit on the croup of the horse. She executed the exercise.

"Now, sit on the neck."

She passed above the pommel. Claire pulled sharply on the rein to force Star's head down, but Amanda did not budge. The little blond girl looked at her with big eyes.

"Aren't you scared?"

"Not at all!"

Sylvan stepped in.

"Come on, that's good enough. Leave her alone!" he told his cousin.

He turned to Amanda.

"Would you like to taste a gallop?"

She shook her head affirmatively. He set the reins in her hands and briefly showed her how to hold them correctly. Then, he turned the animal; its nose against the breeze.

"I'm going to send him," he explained. "He'll naturally go over to the other horses there. If you feel you're losing your balance, let go of the reins and hold onto the mane. Do you understand?"

"I think so!"

He grabbed a handful of hair to demonstrate.

"Alright!" she nodded.

He let out his wild cry. The animal started like a bolt. Amanda, unsettled, let go of the reins and grabbed firmly onto the mane. She felt the rhythm of the animal penetrate her body.

She was thankful for the boy's instructions. The wind delightfully gushed on her face. Amazingly, they had already arrived at the end of the meadow. The horse stopped. Sylvan came running after her, laughing with joy.

"Come, I want to introduce you to my father. If he agrees, you can come back and ride with us."

The three children led her behind the house.

"Papa!"

A tall, handsome man came out of a stable. He wore a cowboy outfit. He smiled at the four, fast-approaching children. His own spoke altogether.

"For God's sake, speak one at a time, please. Julie, introduce your new friend to me."

"Papa, this is Amanda. She loves horses and she can ride. She's been riding Claire's horse. Can she come and play with us?"

The man looked at Amanda, and then turned his back on them.

"Of course, she can. She can come and play with you as much as she likes—but as far as the horses are concerned . . . . "

"What Papa?" Sylvan asked anxiously.

His father sighed and looked back at them.

"It's better that she doesn't ride our horses anymore."

"But Papa, why? She can just—"

His father interrupted him firmly.

"Sylvano! I know it might be difficult for you to understand, but we have no insurance for her; if something happened to her, we would be responsible."

Sylvan and Amanda looked so disappointed; he slipped away.

"What a shame!" the boy exclaimed, upset.

"Thank you all the same! You've been very kind to me. Now, it's time for me to go home."

Sylvan became sullen. He turned around and left without saying goodbye.

She sighed.

The girls accompanied Amanda to the gate. On the way, they tittle-tattled in a manner that made her feel ill at ease.

"Come back to visit!" they said as she climbed onto her bike.

However, Amanda decided she would not go back to play with them.

* * *

That evening, Amanda told her mother about her adventure.

"Maman, I would like so much to go horse riding!"

"I know, Honey, but the lessons and equipment are costly, without talking about how to get you to the ranch."

"I can get there by bike."

"It's about eight kilometers. Anyway, you know we can't afford it. You already play the violin. You must make a choice. It's one or the other."

Amanda remained silent, thinking. She had always wanted to play the violin. She sighed.

"Alright, it'll be the violin."

Her mother smiled, relieved.

That night, as Amanda sank into sleep, she heard Papa singing softly in the kitchen:

"Sweetheart, when the evening sets on the plain
And the nightingale is back to sing again,
When the wind blows on the green heather,
We'll go listen to the song of the golden wheat.
We'll go listen to the song of the golden wheat."[19]

---

19 La Chanson des Blés d'Or, 1880, paroles de Soubise et Lemaître, musique Frédéric Doria.

LA RENTRÉE

AT THE END OF THE SUMMER, when Amanda passed by the mansion, it was closed. The horses were gone. She was eager to start school again. This year she entered middle school as a sixth grader. The evening before the first day of school, at the supper table, she was quiet, which was unusual. This concerned her father.

"Amanda, are you alright?"

"Yes, I'm perfectly fine. I'm just thinking."

"What are you thinking about?"

"I'm thinking about Angela."

"Well, what makes you think about Angela?"

"Every year, it's the same. All the girls avoid her. They say she is dirty and nobody ever greets her with a kiss. Well, sometimes she gets a running nose and it seems she never carries a handkerchief with her. It's a shame because she's not bad, at all. She never bothers anyone and she never complains."

"They're very poor. Since her parents died, her grandmother has been raising her four grandchildren by herself. This poor woman, she has a hard time. She is totally overwhelmed," Louise remarked.

"As for me, I don't mind greeting her with a kiss, when she doesn't have a running nose, of course, but I get the impression she avoids me so as not to create problems."

"What kind of problems?"

"Well, you know, the girls always say mean things when some-one shows some kindness to her. I'd like to set a good example on the first day of school. The problem is, I don't know how to answer them, and this only makes the situation more difficult for Angela."

"Listen," her mother said suddenly. "When I was a little girl, there's one thing we used to say to quiet the others down."

And Louise declaimed a sentence.

"Oh Maman, I'm afraid this is a little too long and outdated."

"Maybe, but it always worked!" she giggled.

★ ★ ★

The middle school was about ten kilometers from Thym, in the bigger village of Bourgeon. The next morning, Amanda joined Jean-Baptiste on the public square by the church to wait for the school bus. Linda was already there, and so were Laura, Perrine, and others.

Valérie would not attend that school. Her parents, rich farmers, had preferred to send her to a boarding school more famous than the middle school of the area.

According to the area custom, Amanda went around the girls for the four regular kisses on both cheeks. Angela had not arrived yet, but Amanda watched for her. When she finally showed up, she was the very last one; she was cleanly dressed, but she stood to the side.

Amanda drew close to her, greeted her, and kissed her like the others. The girl seemed happy and embarrassed at the same time. As soon as they were finished with the usual greetings, the offensive remarks started from every side.

"Are you stupid?"

"Are you crazy? She's gross."

"Who has to kiss her, anyway?"

"Well, why not? She's as human as you or me!"

"You aren't human; you're disgusting. That's what you are!"

"Anyway, you'll never change; you'll always be dense!"
The girls stopped talking. The ball was in Amanda's camp and
they waited for an answer worthy of their dispute. Amanda hesitated, drew her breath, and then spouted, all at once.
"The slime of the toad doesn't reach the white dove! That I am,"
she added, after a second thought.
The girls were so surprised by the response, since it demanded
some kind of thinking. By the time they came back to their senses,
the time for an answer had passed. That is, if there was to be an
answer.
Suddenly, Laura, who had not said a word, moved forward and
kissed Angela on both cheeks. When Perrine, the baker's daughter,
saw her, she was encouraged to do the same. Then, Linda followed,
and finally all of the others. As for Amanda, she was not yet over the
effect her old-fashioned statement had had, when the bus stopped
on the square.
It was a red school bus, decorated with a green stripe that ran
around its entire length. It picked up all the children from the
neighboring farms. They entered through the back, by a two-leaved
door.
Inside, three benches ran along the body of the vehicle—one
against each side and one in the middle. The children on the right
and middle benches faced each other. This bus could hold about
thirty young people.
Aurélie was already there. Amanda chose a place in the back,
next to the door. Jean-Baptiste regained his favorite seat, toward the
front, not far from the driver.
The bus started for the countryside. Two kilometers down the
road it made a left turn and entered a narrow way unraveled between hedgerows. It stopped in front of a farm. Two schoolchildren,
a boy and a girl, came out and quickly climbed into the vehicle.
Amanda's eyes crossed the boy's. Her mouth opened with surprise. It was Sylvan and Julie! He slowly looked away and found a
seat. This first trip was very quiet.

IN THE SCHOOL BUS

AFTER SCHOOL WAS OVER, AMANDA CLIMBED back into the bus. Joël and André had already saved places on the middle bench for themselves and fiercely guarded the seats in front of them. Amanda crept behind them and sat on the left side of the bus.

When Sylvan stepped in, the boys designated a free place to him, right in front of them. Two of the leaders, Yves and Robert, sat on each side of him. They looked odd. As soon as the bus departed, they started to provoke him.

"Hey, new boy, can you fight?"

Sylvan straightened up slowly. His dark eyes narrowed.

He looked around, and then asked, "Who's the leader?"

"I am," André answered, eyeing him from head to foot.

Sylvan stood up and, without any further notice, landed a blow on André's face. As the boy brought his hand to his nose, Joël got up to come to his friend's rescue, but a knee kick welcomed him in the stomach.

Robert and Yves got up as if one man. The new boy had already turned around to face them. The blows started to pour down with baffling rapidity. The other children watched, startled. Yet, the fight was unfair.

André seized Sylvan from behind and managed to immobilize him by closing his right arm on his throat. With his other arm, he

84

held onto the back of the bench, as the bus was speeding over bumps and holes, and threw them around. Sylvan tried to strike backwards with his elbow in the stomach, but André held on tightly.

He shouted, "Hold his arms!"

Robert tried to approach him from the front to seize his left arm, but a kick kept him at a respectful distance and the middle seat did not allow him any space to move to the exact place. During that time, Yves, who was on the right side, managed to seize his right arm and twisted it.

Nonetheless, Sylvan's left arm, on the side of the middle bench, seemed impossible to grab. Right behind, there sat Amanda.

Jacques, who was about two seats higher up, got up. The girl next to Amanda flattened out to let him through. On the contrary, Amanda bent forward and blocked his path.

"Get out of my way!" he ordered.

"That's enough! There's no space for you on the other side," she retorted.

He grabbed her coat and pulled her backwards, but she stretched her legs across his way. He climbed over the back of the middle bench. Robert made space for him, but he had landed too far.

Meanwhile, Sylvan used his free hand to try to pull off the iron grip strangling him, but without any success. He barely managed to turn his head aside and planted his teeth furiously into the arm holding him.

André screamed with pain and released his hold, but Sylvan did not unclench his teeth. André turned pale. Yves let go of the right arm. Sylvan cleared himself free.

Jacques quickly passed over the back of the seat again. The others kept a respectful distance from him. The fight had suddenly ceased.

The winner, staggering, drew a deep breath and blew up on his face, covered with sweat. He passed his fingers through his hair to brush it off his forehead, but it fell right back into place.

"So, who's the leader?" he questioned boldly.

The leaders looked at the floor. André held his arm. They did not dare to answer.

* * *

The bus had arrived at Sylvan's place. As he was about to step out the door, he turned towards Amanda, and looked at her straight in the eyes. He nodded lightly to her. Embarrassed, she looked away. He jumped off the vehicle.

On the square of the church, Amanda found her brother.

"He fights as well as he can ride a horse!" she remarked.

Jean-Baptiste grinned with disgust.

"I hate fights," he said.

* * *

Day after day, morning and evening, Sylvan and Amanda exchanged a quick glance. Julie, the boy's sister, had discovered Laura could be made a scapegoat and decided to take advantage of it. Every evening, at the departure from the school, she started to tease her and pull her hair. Now, the dark side of Julie's character was showing.

Laura was an easy prey because of her little size and her timid temperament. Also, she did not have any big brother to impress others. Amanda felt sorry for her.

One evening, as Julie had grabbed a handful of Laura's hair, she pulled it to force her head to the floor of the bus and held it there until the bus stopped in front of her place. Once she got out, Laura burst into tears. Sylvan, who was still on the bus, saw her. He halted.

"Starting tomorrow, I'll avenge myself of you all; I'll make all the girls cry, one after another," he declared, and then jumped to the ground.

The girls shuddered with horror. If his sister was a torturer, he was a real terror. Amanda, more than anyone else, wondered: *Is he still seeking revenge for the way he was treated on the first day of school, or what?*

Sylvan's attitude was so confusing.

* * *

He held true to his promise. The next day, the bus had barely started when he got up.

"Who am I going to start with?" he wondered aloud.

The girls held their breath.

"You!"

He designated Perrine because she sat in front of him. Several children glanced toward her big brother, but he chose not to interfere.

Sylvan began by pulling a lock of her hair, and then punched her. She started to cry. Different from his sister, he was speedy. Satisfied, he sat down.

"That's one," he said. "Tomorrow, it'll be another."

* * *

The scenario repeated itself day after day and continued into the next week. The boy started by pulling some hair; as soon as he got a grin out of the girl he mistreated, he punched her.

Usually this was enough to make her cry. Sometimes, the girl started to cry before he had even touched her. In that case, he would stop right away—surprised, but delighted.

Meanwhile, the other children enjoyed the entertainment. Only Jean-Baptiste kept away—at the front of the bus, next to the driver.

"If my father were here, that wouldn't happen," he remarked.

"I know your father. He'd get in trouble with a lot of parents," the driver answered. "As far as I'm concerned, as long as there is no blood or broken bones, this is not my business."

His philosophy, similar to the one of the people of that area, was to never interfere in children's internal disputes.

* * *

Finally, only three girls remained who had not yet been subjected to the bully's humiliation. Amanda was among them.

That evening, as she stepped out of the bus, she waited for her brother to join her.

She blurted out, "I hate him; that brute! Linda is not taking the bus anymore because of him."

"How does she get back home from school then?" he asked.

"She stays at her cousins' in Bourgeon and her mother drives her back in the evening after work. As far as Sylvan is concerned, let him come, just let him come to me! I'm going to mess up his handsome nose."

As she spoke, she rubbed her clenched fist.

"If he doesn't provoke you, don't look for him!" Jean-Baptiste advised firmly.

"I know. I won't. I don't understand. Not one of the girls is trying to stand up to him even a little bit, nor are their brothers. Why hasn't he tried messing with me yet? I've been waiting for so long!"

"He probably has a reason."

"A reason? He's scared. That's what he is!"

"I doubt it. That would be rather amazing."

He could not help smiling, teasingly.

"Well, what then?"

Jean-Baptiste bit his lip. He looked at his little sister, but did not answer.

* * *

On Thursday evening, Amanda restlessly waited to ride on the bus. Sylvan did not even look at her. That evening and the next, he only paid attention to the two remaining girls.

Like the others, they did not try anything to defend themselves. They wanted to get through the ordeal as fast as possible. Sylvan had hardly touched them before they began to cry.

Now, it was the weekend and Amanda was enraged.

* * *

On Monday evening, as she was about to step into the bus, a few schoolmates strangely stood in her way.

"Amanda, come here! We have a secret to tell you."

"What secret?"

They pulled her aside.

"Come here, this way, and just wait and see!"

"See what? There's nothing to see."

"It's a secret!"

Other children boarded onto the bus. She realized they merely tried to hold her back outside.

"There's no secret. Come on, let me go!"

However, two boys inside the bus stopped her from entering. When everybody else was on board, and it was finally time to leave, they let her in.

She was the last one, and the last free seat was in the middle of the bus, right in front of Sylvan. He glanced at her. She sat down. The bus started.

He was calm, and did not make a move. A few minutes later, Jacques, who sat next to him, showed signs of restlessness. He turned toward him.

"You said you were going to make all the girls cry," he reminded him.

"I did! So what?"

"There's still one left."

Sylvan's dark eyes rested gently on Amanda. She stared at him harshly. He looked away.

"Come on; it's her turn!" the children shouted. "It is! We want to see it."

"I don't feel like fighting today," Sylvan answered quietly.

"Are you scared of her? You're a scaredy-cat!"

Sylvan did not answer. Jeering and hissing became louder. The shouts came in unison, one rhythm.

"Amanda! Amanda!"

He slowly got up. The voices died down. Amanda tightened her muscles. With fists clenched, she was about to aim at his nose, but he was still too far from her. Clearly she was not afraid of him. In front of her determined look, he could not help smiling briefly, amused.

Suddenly, a voice coming from the front of the bus broke through the silence.

"If you're going to touch my sister, it'll be over my dead body," Jean-Baptiste was standing.

The boy turned toward him.

"Stay where you are, Vissac! In case you didn't hear me, I just said I had no intention to fight tonight. Don't worry! I'm not going to touch your sister."

He defied all the faces turned toward him.

"I'm the leader. I decide!"

He took advantage of a turn in the road to let the bus swing him back into his seat. Apart from Sylvan and Jean-Baptiste, Amanda wondered who—she or her classmates—was the most disappointed.

When the bus arrived at Sylvan's stop, he was about to jump down when he turned around. He looked at her straight in the eyes. She did not look away.

The others started to understand. They did not dare say a word. Sylvan's past actions had already quenched all the teasing possibilities.

* * *

When the bus reached the parking lot by the church, the children exited and quickly dispersed. Jean-Baptiste and Amanda started on their way home, side-by-side. She finally broke the silence.

"Thank you for what you did on the bus, but honestly, you've messed up everything. I've been getting ready for so long . . ."

Jean-Baptiste glanced at her and shook his head.

"It seems you're the only one who doesn't understand anything."

"Understand what?"

"That's what I'm saying; you don't understand a thing."

She blinked.

"What do you mean?"

Jean-Baptiste bit his lip. He tried not to laugh. He started to walk briskly.

"You're not going to like it—" he anticipated.

She was trying to keep up with him.

"Tell me!"

He hastened his pace.

"He loves you!" he explained, and then he took off.

Thanks to the speed of his long legs, there was soon a safe distance between him and his furious, younger sibling.

She shouted, "He's a brute. I hate him!"

She tried to catch up with her brother, but his light hair had totally vanished at the end of the street. Out of breath, she stopped by the tall chestnut trees shading the village recreational hall, a block away from her home.

The air was filled with the sweet and sour smell of dead leaves. She looked up to the great trees, dressed in their fall colors.

Could it be the whole time, Sylvan had been trying to . . . ? Oh là là![20]

Suddenly, the simple scenery became romantic.

---

20 Oh là là!: Oh dear, Oh my!

FIRST COMMUNION

IN THE WIDE KITCHEN, LOUISE PUT her last touch to the evening meal. Her daughter was helping her set the table when Jean-Baptiste came in. He drew close to the stove that heated the whole house, and stretched his hands out above the burning plate to warm them up.

"So," asked their mother, "what's new?"

"We don't see Sylvan and Julie anymore," Amanda remarked.

"That's right," her brother added, "and you can be happy, for we *won't* see them anymore."

"Why?" asked their mother. "Were they that bad?"

Jean-Baptiste let his sister answer. She shrugged.

"I was just starting to get used to them."

"I heard their parents placed them in a boarding school," Jean-Baptiste informed.

"How do you know that?"

"That's what's going around."

"Well, since they've gone, Linda said she would take the bus with us again, and this is nice. Every day we can walk back home together. Since we're also in the same class, she has become my best friend."

"I saw her grandmother last week," Louise stepped in. "She's so glad you invited Linda to go to catechism with you. That way, you'll also do your communion together."

"I showed Linda the picture Bible you gave me," Amanda went on excitedly, "and you know what? She asked her parents for a Bible for Christmas. Now, she's got her own Bible, too!"

Armand Vissac appeared in the kitchen. He took off his beret. "Bonsoir! Have you heard the news?"

All faces turned to him.

"There's just been a terrible accident by Bourgeon. I heard that was left of the car was about as flat as an iron sheet. Inside the car were four young people. Two of them were Bechar boys."

Amanda opened her mouth, but there was a heavy silence.

"Two of Linda's cousins . . ." she finally uttered painfully. "This is terrible."

"I just saw her grandmother. She said not to wait for your friend tomorrow morning. Her mother will drive her to school."

* * *

The next day, when Amanda arrived at the school, Linda's mother had just dropped her off. The poor girl had swollen eyes from having cried so much. As soon as her mother disappeared, she started to sob again.

Amanda got close to her, but she could not find any words to comfort Linda, so she just stood there, by her side. When her friend started for their classroom—her face hidden in her hands—Amanda followed. Linda spent the whole first hour of class, sobbing.

The next course was French. The children got in line to change classrooms. The French teacher noticed the grieving girl in the back of the row—her face buried in her hands. Tears ran through her fingers.

"My God, this is terrible," she exclaimed. "This child is really too upset."

Amanda still stood by Linda. So, the teacher—obviously over-whelmed—unexpectedly turned to Amanda.

"You! Do something. I don't know, but don't let her be like this."

"Madame!" she answered. "There is nothing to do. She's been crying like this all morning."

"This would worry me."

The teacher made a quick decision.

"Children, you wait for me here. I can't keep her like this. She ought to be sent back home."

She grabbed Linda by the shoulders and led her away. Amanda leaned against the wall. She was relieved.

* * *

Back home, Amanda had just received a bookmark from her grandfather. On it the Ten Commandments were written. She meditated upon them, and then entered the kitchen, the bookmark in her hand.

"Maman, in the Ten Commandments, God says He is a jealous God. If God is perfect, how can He be jealous? I've always been told jealousy was bad."

"Well, tomorrow is Wednesday. You can ask your teacher at catechism."

"This is a good idea. I will."

* * *

The next day, Amanda waited patiently for the end of the class to ask her question. The teacher took the bookmark, looked at it closely, and turned it around.

"Wait a minute," she said. "I'll be back."

She went into another room to talk to the priest, and then came back, the bookmark in her hand.

"You shouldn't read these kinds of things," she said severely.

"My grandfather gave it to me," the girl protested.

"It's all the same. You shouldn't read this."

"Why not?"

"Because there are things in there you can't understand."

"Well, will you explain it to me?"

"I can't either. It's up to the priest to do that."

Amanda reached out. The teacher handed the bookmark back to her. She seized it and buried it in her pocket. She left the room, furious.

* * *

Back home, she shared her disappointment with her mother.

"Not only did she not give me any answer to my question, but she put Pépère into question!"

Her mother tried to comfort her.

"Don't be so upset over such a little matter. Humans don't have an answer for everything. That's that."

* * *

Easter time drew near. One Wednesday, the priest decided to take the catechism children to the church to view the Stations of the Cross portrayed in scenes that hung around the square-stone walls of the thirteenth century edifice. They stepped from the warmth of the spring sun into the coolness of the tall and silent building. The smell of incense and burned candles mixed together, adding its touch to the religious atmosphere.

Before starting, the priest prepared his catechumens with a few explanations.

"You're going to see, in each picture, the sufferings of Jesus Christ as He was going to the cross. Now, please, don't get upset about that. There is no reason to get upset, as all this is in the past."

Once they finished going around the church, the priest asked them to sit quietly for a time of meditation. Amanda sighed; her heart heavy with questions.

On the way back home, she turned to Linda, who accompanied her, silently.

"Why did Jesus have to die on the cross?" she asked. "Do you understand that?"

Without waiting for an answer, she went on, "Why shouldn't we be upset about that? It was awful. He hadn't done anything wrong, had He? Or is it just an old, dusty story?"

Linda had not quite gotten used to her strange friend yet. Hesitant, she did not answer. Suddenly, Amanda felt inspired.

"I know. I've got it. This is the very reason why we're going to do our communion. The day of our communion, God will certainly answer all of our questions. We'll be like . . . enlightened. Don't you think so?"

Linda shrugged.

She finally said, "I don't understand very well what you're trying to say, but it's okay. Au revoir!"

Their paths separated.

"See you tomorrow!"

* * *

Amanda's grandparents and her Tante Mimi, who was also her godmother, came from Belfort for her communion. Her godfather came also, from Haute-Loire. Her grandfather offered her a jewel box he had created for her. Her father took some pictures of her and Linda in their white dresses, but Amanda felt utterly disappointed. When she had taken the communion bread, she had had no revelation.

In the days that followed, her mother found her a couple of times on her bed, crying. She started to worry.

"What's wrong, Honey? You just don't seem like yourself anymore."

"I'm okay, Maman, nothing serious. I'll be fine."

Louise tried to insist a little more, but she was not able to get anything else out of her daughter. Amanda would have died rather than admit, to herself or anyone else, she no longer believed in God. She felt miserable.

THE GENDARME'S DAUGHTER

THE GEOGRAPHY TEACHER DISTRIBUTED RELIEF MAPS of Europe. At the top of her paper, Amanda wrote her name and the name of her new class: 5ème C.[21]

The teacher asked the students to color the map with different colors, according to the elevations. Amanda was embarrassed, for she had forgotten her crayons. She just sat quietly, hoping the teacher would not notice her, when a classmate to her right discreetly whistled to her.

"Tsk . . ."

She glanced over. A tall blond girl, with twinkling eyes, tried to get her attention. She held up her crayons and indicated she wanted to pass them over to her. Amanda, surprised, did not react right away, but the girl insisted. She finally smiled back, lightly, and nodded, affirmatively.

The young lady observed the teacher closely. As soon as his attention was safely turned away from them, she passed a handful of crayons to her neighbor. Amanda used them sparingly, and then returned them to their owner when the time seemed favorable. The blond girl smiled, broadly, at her.

Amanda looked at her watch. Impatiently, she waited for the end of the class so she might get to know this new friend better,

---

21 7th grade C.

during recess. As soon as the bell rang, she jumped off her seat.

"Salut, what's your name?"

"I'm Miriam. And what's your name?"

"Amanda. Where are you from?"

"I'm from here."

Amanda could not help, but to look disappointed.

"Well! I assume you have plenty of friends then."

"Don't I wish!" the girl answered derisively.

She seemed to always be smiling, however, as if life were a big joke. She got up and sat down on her desktop.

Amanda frowned.

"You don't seem that bad off."

"Oh no, it's not me. It's just my father. I mean . . . he isn't bad, he just—"

She interrupted herself and bit her lip. Josie, Sophie, and Chantal had surrounded her and approached close enough to pressure her.

"Come on, say it. Tell her what your father does!"

"You aren't ashamed of him, are you?"

Miriam tried to get up and escape.

"Don't blockade me!" she warned. "No, I've never been ashamed of my father."

The girls in front of her were not allowing her to break through. From behind her, Amanda grabbed her arm and tried to pull her back.

"What did you want to tell me?" she asked.

Miriam sharply cleared off her arm.

"This is not the time. It's easy to tell you're not from here."

"Well . . . it seems you don't have much choice. I'd rather hear the facts from you than from them," Amanda answered carefully, pointing to the pack.

While the other girls sneered, Miriam calmed down and scrutinized her, hesitant.

"You really want to know!"

"Now, that you've started, it's better to finish," her new friend encouraged.

"Alright, my father is a gendarme and part of his job is to give fines. This is why they don't like me."

"And . . . is that all?" Amanda asked with relief.

"That's all," the young lady's face relaxed with a teasing smile.

"I like gendarmes," Amanda declared boldly. "My father says they make sure the law is respected."

"Would you say the same thing, if her father had given *your* father a fine?" Josie snapped.

"Oh, you mean your father doesn't respect the law?"

Josie opened her mouth and closed it. Amanda went on.

"Her father is only doing his job; that's all. In any case, there is no reason to involve Miriam."

"Be quiet! Come along," Miriam ordered abruptly.

Amanda obeyed.

The other girls started away resentful, grumbling, "Qui se ressemble s'assemble."[22]

Once they were left alone, Amanda asked, "Why did you want me to be quiet? Did I say anything wrong?"

"You don't know them, but they can be really mean. I don't want you to get into trouble because of me."

Amanda shrugged.

"Don't worry. I'm not afraid of them."

The blue eyes twinkled again.

"Just tell me, where are you from?"

"I'm from Thym."

"It seems, to me, you don't know many people in this class."

"You're right. I feel rather lonely. My best friend is in another class this year and . . . I hadn't noticed you yet."

"Well . . . Want to be my friend?"

"Do I want to!"

---

22 "Birds of a feather flock together."

* * *

Not long after, during a teacher's sick leave, Miriam invited Amanda to the gendarmes' local compound. As the young ladies passed by the guards' office, they got a glimpse of a man wearing handcuffs while being photographed from different angles.

Amanda stopped, fascinated, but Miriam pulled her away. She wanted to introduce her to her mother.

The two girls entered a plain, but clean home. A dimpled lad, with blond locks, welcomed them joyfully.

"This is my little brother," Miriam stated proudly. "You already know my big brother from school."

"Yes, and I also know your little sister from school, for they all look so much like you!"

"I have two other little sisters you don't know. Come in, here's mother."

A woman watched television and knitted a bi-colored sweater at the same time. She turned around.

"Mother, I want to introduce thee to my best friend from school, Amanda."

"Bonjour, Mademoiselle."

"Bonjour, Madame."

Her friend's mother watched a police series.

"Look," she exclaimed, "I'm sure this is the bad guy!"

"How can you watch TV, guess the bad guy, and knit with two different threads at the same time?" Amanda marveled.

The lady's eyes twinkled.

"It's just a question of habit," she answered, simply.

"Mother knits all our sweaters," Miriam added. "She did this one!"

She pointed to the bright, gold-and-brown sweater she wore.

"Mother, do thou mind if I show Amanda pictures of my other sisters?"

"Just make sure you put them back."

"I will."

As the girls headed to Miriam's room, Amanda whispered, "Why were you teasing your mother?"

"I wasn't, was I?"

"Well, you told her 'thou' when you talked to her."

"We've always said 'thou' to our parents," she answered, her eyes twinkling, as usual.

"You aren't serious, are you?"

"Yes, I am."

Miriam made a big effort to just look serious, but she could not keep her eyes from twinkling.

"Alright, I believe you. Actually you might think I'm peculiar, too. Do you know we've never had a TV in our home?"

"You've got to be kidding."

"Not at all, I'm serious."

It was Amanda's turn to try to look serious. Both girls soon giggled again.

* * *

As the two friends headed back to school, Philippe, a boy from their classroom, welcomed them very warmly.

"Salut, girls! Would you please kiss me?"

"Are you alright? You've got to be crazy!"

"I'm not. Rather, let me explain to you. We've organized a kiss competition."

"A what?"

"Yes, you heard me well! The boy, who receives a kiss from the greatest number of girls from the whole 7th grade section, wins."

"Berck!"

"Gross!"

"How disgusting . . . ."

Philippe looked very hurt. Laurent had just joined him.

"Come on, it's not that bad!" he urged. "You can't imagine how much you would be helping us."

"You two are the only ones left to determine the winner."

Miriam and Amanda looked at each other. Other boys ran up to their competitors from all directions.

"You poor things," one of the girls mocked.

"This is your problem," the other one added. "We didn't invent that stupid game."

"And don't come too close or I'll call my brother," Miriam warned, to close the subject.

The boys moved away, disappointed. They already passed the word there was no hope as far as these two were concerned.

"Miriam," Amanda declared, solemnly, "you're a *real friend.*"

"Come on!" Miriam answered simply.

She wrapped her arm around Amanda's shoulders and they started for their classroom.

* * *

M. Leduc, the physical education teacher had barely come back from his military service. He was tough with the girls. One day, he took them out for a cross-country run.

"Today," he explained, "we're going to cover several kilometers, but we have to be back here within one hour. Go!"

"Horrors, we're not in the army, are we?" Miriam grumbled.

Amanda laughed. As the group started running, she took its lead. Soon, Miriam held her side. Amanda slowed down. Then, as soon as her friend caught up with her, she went back to her pace. The teacher pushed the speed from the rear. He did not allow the stragglers any rest.

"Come on Amanda, slow down!" Josie and Sophie begged.

She did not answer. She kept the lead, leaving a fair distance between her and the pack. Miriam, who did not want to find herself with the others, had, now, caught her rhythm.

After twenty minutes, M. Leduc ordered a rest. All around, the freshly ploughed fields stretched as far as the eye could see. A strong smell of damp earth filled the air.

Within the group, tension continued to grow.

"I hate them!" some girls grumbled about the two friends.

The teacher gave the signal for departure.

"Amanda! You keep the lead!" he ordered.

"Non Monsieur! S'il vous plait Monsieur! Not her!" the girls strongly protested. "She runs crazy!"

"I'm the one in charge, and I'm in command!" was his final answer.

Amanda had already started.

"You'll see when we arrive," the girls shouted to her. "We'll have a little celebration for you."

"I'm afraid that is true," Miriam panted. "They're so mean."

"Be quiet and run," her friend replied.

The two girls arrived five minutes before the end of the allotted time. One-by-one, the other girls straggled in. They gathered together on the sports ground when the bell for recess, rang.

The teacher, along with the last of the crew, had not come in yet; however, Josie, Sophie, and Chantal had arrived. They came up to Amanda and encircled her threateningly.

"You're going to pay for that, you dirt!"

"Easy! What wrong did I do to you?"

"Don't you realize how you made us run?"

"I didn't make you run!"

"Mademoiselle Vissac wanted to be the first, right?"

"So what? Is there anything wrong with that?"

Miriam took her by the arm and tried to pull her away.

"Come, let's get out of here!" she urged her.

Amanda resisted.

"Wait a minute! I can't believe I can't reason with them."

"You can't argue with them, they're—"

"You, stay out of this!" Chantal interrupted. "Besides, as to your friend, we're going to destroy her!"

Josie raised her hand. Miriam pulled Amanda sharply backwards and stepped in front of her. She clenched her teeth. A burning slap struck her, right across the face. Tears filled her eyes.

At that very moment, the teacher arrived. He took in the whole scene, but did not intervene. When the girls saw him, they calmed down right away. Amanda seized her friend by the shoulder and dragged her away.

"Monsieur—" she started.

"Just drop it!" Miriam cut her short.

She took her friend by the arm and pulled her out of the sports ground.

"Miriam! You're alright?"

The young lady gingerly pressed her fingers to her cheek.

"He saw everything. Leduc saw it all! Why don't you want me to speak to him?"

Two familiar dimples appeared on Miriam's face. Her humid eyes twinkled again. She looked like a rainbow after a storm.

"It's useless. My father gave him a fine yesterday. I know that."

"Oh . . . this is so unfair." Amanda moaned.

BELFORT

IN THE MIDDLE OF WINTER, SIX hundred kilometers east of Thym, as the city of Belfort was covered with snow, Pépère and Mémère had just gotten up for the day. The warm smell of coffee filled their little apartment. Before starting breakfast, Pépère bowed his head, as he did every morning, and prayed.

". . . We also want to pray for the Vissac family: for our children and grandchildren. Put your hand particularly on our grandson, Jean-Baptiste, and also our granddaughter, Amanda, today, and also bring them to you . . . ."

"Amen," said Mémère at the end.

* * *

Amanda loved her history and geography class. However, what she especially liked was the teacher, M. Gilet. He was good, serious, and drew the respect of his students. This year, the culture of ancient Egypt was part of the program. That day, the class had started rather poorly.

The children were excited and M. Gilet had to call the class back to order. Still, he did not regain his usual calm. He had brought a projector and showed some slides about Egypt, including the pyramids, tombs, Pharaohs, sacred objects of ritual, and mummies.

Then, he turned off the projector. He went back to his place in the front of the class and started to write on the board.

"What is a mummy? The Egyptians of that time believed there was a life after death. Therefore, they embalmed the body with fragrant herbs to preserve it, carefully wrapped it with strips of white cloth, and laid it down in a tomb with objects from daily life and food so the person could still eat after death."

A few students thought this was funny and started to laugh. Someone even sang softly, "Mummy, mummy . . . ."

M. Gilet turned around sharply. They all became silent. He turned back to the blackboard and rapidly drew a cross on it. Then, he looked back at them again. He was upset.

"Do you think your Christ on the cross makes any more sense than a living mummy? Christ is no better than a mummy!"

Amanda breathed rapidly. She clenched her teeth. He did not have the right to say so!

Nevertheless, nobody dared to challenge him.

* * *

That night, Amanda undressed slowly. Through her bedroom window, the light of the moon poured down on her. There was no shutter and she had not pulled the curtains yet. She slid into her pajamas and drew close to the windowpane.

The moon was full. It was enormous—beautiful. She stared intensely into the sky. She breathed.

"God, where are you?"

Her teacher's sentence still resounded painfully in her head.

"Christ is no better than a mummy!"

She reached her bed and laid down on her back, her eyes wide open.

"God, I didn't defend You. I'm sorry for that, but to tell You the truth, I don't believe in You anymore. Well, if You exist, You already know that. How about if You don't exist? How am I going to know? You understand that—if You don't exist—I have no time to waste on You. If You don't exist, what's the point in believing in You? Now, if You do exist . . . boy! I'm lost, just because I don't believe in You."

A light sweat covered her face.

"God, I'm scared . . . I'm scared of dying. If I die now, and You exist, I'm not ready . . . You'll send me to hell . . . just because I don't believe in You."

Tears filled her eyes. She sat up, grabbed her pillow, and buried her face into it. She felt like she was falling into a deep black hole without end, and she sobbed.

After a while, she calmed down, exhausted. She removed the pillow from her face so she could breathe. A few Bible verses, heard at church, came back to her memory.

"God, it's written in Your Word—You are love. If this is true, don't let me die before I know You. You also said the one who seeks shall find, and You would open to the one who knocks. Well, if You do exist, please, listen to me. I commit myself to seeking You alright, but You have to do Your part. I need You to reveal Yourself to me. I can't do it myself."

Amanda felt she had made a fair deal with God. It was good enough for the day. Her breathing became normal, and she peacefully fell asleep.

* * *

The second trimester of school was coming to an end. The teacher, M. Gilet, had just read aloud the final average mark of each student for the last three months. Amanda's average had gone down by one mark compared to the previous term. Marie had taken first place.

The students slowly left the room. M. Gilet had already left and Amanda was still working on putting her things away when Marie turned to her and defied her.

"Well, you see, I'm better than you!"

Amanda shrugged.

"I never said I was the best."

"Just admit it hurts that I've passed you."

Amanda turned around. The blond girl sat on her desk like a queen. She would have been pretty if she had not hidden her eyes and face under a thick layer of makeup. Amanda was impressed by it as the girl was not yet thirteen years old.

"I wish you knew how little I care about that!" she answered.

"Why, then, did you get a fifteen average at the end of the first term?"

"Because I was able to."

"You must be disappointed then."

"Maybe, but not because of you; I don't care about your marks. All I care about is what I can do."

"Meanwhile, I'm the best."

Amanda chose to keep quiet, but Philippe and Laurent had not missed one single word of the exchange.

"You're wrong," Philippe stepped in, suddenly. "You're not the best. Amanda is the best."

Marie looked shocked.

"Oh!"

Amanda was embarrassed.

"Marie had the best average this term," she remarked.

"Just be quiet!" Laurent interrupted her.

"That's right," Philippe continued. "To us, it doesn't make any difference what marks Marie gets. You're the best and you always will be."

Marie pinched her lips.

"You've got to prove it."

"This is easy," Laurent proposed. "There is still one term left. The one that finishes the best average wins."

"I bet on Amanda," Philippe declared.

Amanda gave the boys a dark look. She picked up her schoolbag and quickly got out of the class.

"Good bye!" she said.

* * *

The Easter vacation began.

Louise accompanied Jean-Baptiste and Amanda to her parents' in Belfort. After several hours on the train, as they started to see the blue ridge of the Vosges Mountains, Louise got excited.

"We're getting closer."

They were shortly thereafter surrounded by mountains. Half an hour later, the children were staring through the windowpane—their eyes wide open—as the train entered the pink fortified city of Belfort. They knew they had only one second to spot the pink citadel overlooking the city and, if they were fast enough, they would get a glimpse of the proud Lion of Belfort[23] stretching its twenty-two meters of pink sandstones right under it.

When they finally entered their grandparents' apartment, delicious smells of Kugelhopf,[24] petits fours,[25] and blueberry pies welcomed them.

"Mémère, you're the best cook in the whole world!" Jean-Baptiste exclaimed as he disappeared into the kitchen.

"When are we going to see the cousins?" Amanda asked her grandfather, right away.

"They're going to leave on vacation soon," he answered.

She was disappointed.

"Are we going to see them, then?"

"They're going to stop by tonight, just before their departure. Your cousin, Mélissa, wants to see you very badly, but they won't stay long. Tomorrow, they'll have a long journey."

---

23. A sculpture by Frédéric Bartholdi, sculptor of the Statue of Liberty in New York, located in Belfort, France.

24 Yeast cake, specialty of Alsace

25 Little cookies

"Pépère, will you take me to church?"

"Of course, I will."

"I mean every Sunday until we leave!"

Her grandfather laughed with delight.

"I don't know about that, but we'll certainly go at least once."

"No, twice!"

He looked at the young one. She was awfully serious.

* * *

The doorbell rang. The cousins came in. The Frey family filled the little apartment to overflowing. Romain, who was now sixteen, was a handsome young man, but his blue eyes were still twinkling with teasing. He warm-heartedly kissed his cousins. After a cheerful welcome, Mélissa and Amanda begged Tante Mimi to allow them to seek refuge in her bedroom. She consented, provided the girls would not sit on her bed and mess up the cover.

They solemnly promised, and then Mélissa pulled Amanda into Tante Mimi's bedroom still untouched. The two girls looked at each other like two conspirators, giggling.

"Should we close the door?"

"Sure! We won't let anyone in!"

A little intimacy felt good. As the night settled in, Mélissa turned the desk lamp on and sat on the carpet, Indian-style. Amanda leaned her back against the bed and stretched her legs on the floor.

"Amanda, I'm so sorry we're leaving on vacation just when you're coming to visit."

"What a shame!"

"I wanted to talk to you so much."

"And I've been waiting for this time for so long!"

"Listen, it's better than nothing. I'll come back in a week. We'll be here on Easter Monday!"

"We go back home the next day!"

Mélissa sighed.

"I know."

"Well, you wanted to talk to me?" Amanda questioned.

"Yes, I did, but maybe we could pray first."

"Alright, you pray!"

Mélissa glanced at her, surprised, and closed her eyes.

"Dear Lord, thank you for bringing us together again. Bless our time together. Bless my dear cousin, Amanda. Amen."

They looked at each other gravely.

"Do you still pray, Amanda?"

Amanda made an effort to be honest.

"That can happen."

"Where are you with the Lord?"

Troubled, she did not answer right away. Mélissa waited.

"I don't know what to tell you," she finally confessed. "I feel so confused, myself, about it."

"Are you saved?"

"Well, one must believe in Jesus Christ to be saved."

"Yes, it's simple enough."

"No, it isn't. It's difficult. Last year, the day of my communion, I was awfully disappointed. I was hoping to meet with God that day, but nothing happened. Then . . . there's this teacher I really like. He's a Communist. I know he doesn't have the right to, but he said Jesus wasn't any better than a mummy."

"You mean you don't believe anymore?"

Mélissa looked so grieved Amanda did not answer directly.

"Look, Mélissa! I'm not finished with God yet."

"I pray for you, you know," her cousin answered softly.

"I know. Don't stop. But . . . you wanted to tell me something."

At that very moment, Oncle Jacques called loudly.

"Mélissa, where are you? We're leaving."

"I've got to go. Sorry. I'll tell you next time. We'll have more time together to talk about important matters."

"Just don't forget."

"I won't. I promise."

PÉPÈRE

THAT FIRST SUNDAY AT HER GRANDPARENTS, Amanda went to church, but it did not do any good. However, she was determined to take advantage of this vacation to sort out a few questions. Her grandfather was reading in the living room. She tiptoed in and sat on the couch. He looked up and stared at her above his glasses.

"Would you like something?"

"Oui, Pépère. I would like to ask you a question."

"Go ahead, mon petit; I'm listening."

Amanda just loved it when Pépère called her "my little one." He turned his chair to face her.

"Did you do your communion?"

"Did I do my communion?" he exclaimed, laughing. "You know, this is a good question. I can't answer you in one sentence, though. It'll take some explanation."

"Did you do it or not?"

"Be patient: I'm going to tell you how it all happened."

Pépère became serious; he thought for a second, and then transported his granddaughter, through imagination, back to Paris, in 1915.

"When I was six years old, my mother became very ill with the Spanish flu. At that time, my father was with the army, on the

French front, in a war against Germany. The family sent him a message: 'Wife terminally ill.' He asked for permission to leave, but it was granted to him only a week later. When he arrived, my mother was dead."

"Do you remember her?"

The eyes of the old man became misty.

"I sure do. She was a very gentle person. I missed her a lot. After that, my father was never the same. He started to drink from grief. The family then decided to send me to my grandparents—to the countryside. There I went to school . . . and the rest of the time, I watched the goats."

He smiled.

"I was tough. I got into mischief many times. One day, a child had brought a prune to school. I never had a prune, before. My grandparents were very poor. So, I stole it and ate it. The maître guessed it was I. He sat me on the top of his big desk, in front of the whole class, and threatened to open my belly if I didn't admit it. I was scared to death, and I started to cry. I finally said, 'C'est moi, M'sieur.'"

Moved, Amanda could imagine the little boy.

"Then, my grandmother punished me. She had a long stick and aimed it at my calves, but she was old; I always managed to jump above the stick."

He got up to demonstrate with his long skinny legs. The whole floor shook. Amanda burst out laughing. Mémère passed her head by the door.

"Louis!" she exclaimed.

He sat right back down. Pépère was gifted in taking people from tears to laughter.

"This is why, when the time came to do my communion, the priest of the village simply refused to have anything to do with me."

Amanda's mouth opened wide, with surprise.

"So you didn't do your communion!"

"Just wait! I'm not finished yet. My father was from a good family and it was important to my aunts that I should do my communion: the honor of the family was at stake. So, they traveled from Paris to talk to that priest. He finally agreed to give me the communion for a large sum of money."

"So you did your communion!"

Her grandfather did not answer; his eyes were lost in rêverie. Amanda tried to bring him back to reality.

"Pépère, what did you feel when you took the communion?"

He sighed.

"You want to know everything, don't you?"

"I do, especially this part."

"Well, I remember when the priest handed me the bread . . . I spat on him. I kicked him in the shin, and I ran away, out of the church."

"You did that?" Amanda was shocked.

"Yes, I did," he answered with a sheepish voice.

"You didn't believe in God, then?"

"That's right, I didn't. I considered myself to be an atheist until the age of fifty. My greatest regret is I didn't come to know the Lord earlier. Maybe I would have made different choices then. Better late than never, and this was His way for me."

"Oh, Pépère!"

Amanda got up, threw her arms around his neck, and kissed him.

"You know your grandmother and me . . . we pray for you."

"Oui, Pépère, I know. Mélissa prays for me, too. She told me."

* * *

Amanda lay on her camping cot, thinking. From her grandfather's story, she had learned two things.

She repeated: "Better late than never, and better earlier than later."

She sighed.

What to do?

She got up. Her grandmother was in the living room, knitting.

"Mémère, where is Pépère?"

"He's in the attic, working on something."

"May I go see him?"

"Of course, you may. I'm sure he'll be happy to see you."

Amanda climbed the stairs that led under the roof of the building. She followed the sound of light hammerings and found herself in front of a long row of doors.

"Pépère!"

"I'm over here!"

The warm fragrance of different woods welcomed her. The place was tiny, but Pépère had golden fingers. He was carving the famous Lion of Belfort out of a piece of wood. She observed him a few minutes, silently. Each stroke was extremely precise.

"Pépère, how did you become a Christian?"

Her grandfather's hammer remained suspended in the air.

"It happened through your mother. She met with some missionaries: the Bergerons. You know them, some. Monsieur Bergeron asked to meet with me, so we invited him here, at home. He explained the gospel and I became a Christian."

He placed his chisel at a special angle and gave a little tap with the hammer.

"Is that all, just like that?"

He blew on a chip.

"Of course, not; there was a lot of internal conflict. I was proud, but finally, I surrendered."

He straightened up and started to sing softly, beating the rhythm; his chisel in one hand and his hammer in the other:

"Just as I am, without one plea,
But that Thy blood was shed for me,
And that Thou bidd'st me come to Thee,
O Lamb of God, I come! I come!"[26]

Then he bent back on his piece of art.
"Come on, go play."
As she moved away, she heard the soft voice starting again. She stopped to listen.

"Just as I am, though tossed about
With many a conflict, many a doubt;
Fighting and fears within, without,
O Lamb of God, I come! I come!"

---

26 "Just As I Am" by Charlotte Elliott, 1835.

EASTER SERVICE

IT WAS EASTER SUNDAY. IN THE church, Amanda sat between Pépère and Mémère, waiting eagerly for the beginning of the worship service. However, she was disappointed, for the pastor of the church was not there. She liked him. Instead, there was a guest speaker.

The service began with the congregation singing "Thine Be the Glory" set to Handel's majestic music. After other songs, and the customary prayers, the visiting preacher stepped up into the pulpit.

"This morning, I would like to acquaint you with a few reasons—objections that have been offered ever since the resurrection of Jesus Christ—for not believing in Him. Then, I will give you the reasons why I'm sure He *is* alive today."

In two sentences, that man had won the full attention of a thirteen-year-old girl.

"It all started with the Jews and Romans. Let's read together in the Gospel of Matthew 27: 62–66[27]:

> *Now on the next day, the day after the preparation, the chief*
> *priests and the Pharisees gathered together with Pilate, and*
> *said, "Sir, we remember that when He was still alive that*

---

27   All Scriptures mentioned in this chapter are taken from the New American Standard Bible, published by Zondervan

> deceiver said, 'After three days I am to rise again.' Therefore,
> give orders for the grave to be made secure until the third day,
> otherwise His disciples may come and steal Him away and
> say to the people, 'He has risen from the dead,' and the last
> deception will be worse than the first." Pilate said to them,
> "You have a guard; go, make it as secure as you know how."
> And they went and made the grave secure, and along with the
> guard they set a seal on the stone.

"Let's read further in the Gospel of Matthew 28: 2–4:

> And behold, a severe earthquake had occurred, for an angel of
> the Lord descended from heaven and came and rolled away the
> stone and sat upon it. And his appearance was like lightning,
> and his clothing as white as snow. The guards shook for fear
> of him and became like dead men.

"Finally, we'll read from verse 11–15 of that same chapter:

> Some of the guard came into the city and reported to the chief
> priests all that had happened. And when they had assembled
> with the elders and consulted together, they gave a large sum
> of money to the soldiers, and said, "You are to say, 'His disci-
> ples came by night and stole Him away while we were asleep.'
> "And if this should come to the governor's ears, we will win
> him over and keep you out of trouble." And they took the
> money and did as they had been instructed; and this story was
> widely spread among the Jews, and is to this day."

The young preacher paused, and then went on, "The Jews and
Romans, together, set a device to make sure resurrection would be
out of the picture. However, life is stronger than death. The resurrection happened. Jesus is alive and nothing has been able to hold
Him back. Why, then, did the world of that time unite to deny the

truth? From the scriptures we just read, I can find at least three main reasons.

"The first is highlighted in the Gospel of John 3:19: *The Light has come into the world, and men loved the darkness rather than the Light, for their deeds were evil.* The refusal of the truth comes from man's pride. Let's not forget the Jews and Romans, together, had just committed a serious crime. They had just condemned and executed an innocent. This is called murder, and moreover, the murder was of God's Anointed One.

"Now, it might be asking too much that they should recognize they had made a terrible mistake—even they, the Pharisees, the righteous ones according to the law! This would be too painful. Just think. It's easier to hide the truth from oneself and others. Truly, pride and cowardice united. What a tragedy!

"We find the second reason lies with the Roman soldiers. They are afraid. However, they had done their duty, properly. They were simply faced with a situation that was far beyond them. They were overwhelmed; at first, they told the truth. If they were not believed, that would mean serious trouble for them. They would be accused of professional incompetence before the governor, but they were relieved.

"They were informed what was important was not what had really happened but, rather, what the Pharisees would have liked to happen. All they had to do was to make up a story that sounded reasonable. Fear and cowardice came together. What a tragedy!

"The third reason is also very human. If the soldiers agree to lie, not only will the Jews give them protection in case of trouble, but on the top of that, they're offering them a large sum of money. Oh, money. Now, the situation is becoming interesting. The love of the world! Lies and money came together. What a tragedy! There's nothing new in that."

As the preacher paused again before going on to his next argument, Amanda was literally memorizing the words of life that flowed out of his mouth, words she had ached to hear for such a long time. And how long would it be before she would hear another sermon?

"Jesus is alive! Human pride, fear, and lies have never been able to keep the Lord Jesus in the tomb. Do you realize what happened to Jesus occurred exactly as the prophets had announced? We still have all their prophecies. They're in our Old Testament. They're the Jewish scriptures. All we have to do is check into them.

"From Adam to Jesus, the coming of the Savior has been announced. Jesus has fulfilled all the signs—from His birth in Bethlehem to His death on the cross. When David predicted His hands and feet would be pierced, it was one thousand years before Jesus appeared. Rome did not even exist yet, and the Roman torture of the crucifixion, even less. How would David have known about it? This was a sign from God, written to be recognized and feed our faith. God never intended for us to believe from nothing. The resurrection was predicted, also.

"Just as an example, I'll read to you from Isaiah 53: *He was cut off out of the land of the living (v.8)* . . . *If He would render Himself as a guilt offering, He will see His offspring, He will prolong His days (v. 10)* . . .

"Some people even go to the point of denying the historicity of Christ, or they assimilate Him as being a normal human being, only a little bit different. Why, then, are we in the year of 1975 if nothing happened nearly two thousand years ago? Have you ever wondered why we have four Gospels; not just one?

"We have various documents narrating the history of the ancient times. However, I don't know of any historical event for which four different historians wrote, each one giving his account. To find only two different authors for one story is an achievement.

"Today, in 1975, we still have four, distinct witnesses of the resurrection event. How can we still doubt? Jesus is alive! Why would thousands of men and women, as well as a coward and liar named Peter, give their lives for a dead imposter? If a martyr church is still very much alive, today, it is because Christ also is alive.

"I'll give you one last reason why I believe in Jesus. I've met

Him personally and He saved me. You can meet Him the same way, but you'll have to leave your pride and fear behind. You'll have to leave behind a love for the world and its lies. However, this renunciation is all worth it; for your allegiance is not to a dead man, but for the risen Christ. Here is what He said concerning us: *I am the resurrection and the life; he who believes in Me will live even if he dies, and everyone who lives and believes in Me will never die. Do you believe this?* (John 11:25–26) Jesus is alive!"

The preacher closed his Bible. The assembly stood up to sing:

> "He lives; He lives; Christ Jesus lives today!
> He walks with me and talks with me
> Along life's narrow way.
> He lives, He lives; salvation to impart!
> You ask me how I know He lives.
> He lives within my heart."[28]

* * *

The worship service had come to the end. Pépère turned to Amanda.

"So, did you like it?"

Her eyes shone.

"He said so many things! I need a little bit of time to think about it. I've got to put some order in my head."

Her grandfather laughed.

"Come, I'm going to introduce you to somebody you don't know yet."

He led her to a corner of the room, toward a little old lady.

"This is my granddaughter, the daughter of Louise," Pépère said proudly.

---

28 "He Lives" by Alfred Henry Ackley, 1933.

Amanda loved it when he introduced her that way. The old Christian lady wobbled on her legs. She smiled at the child.

"Bonjour, Mademoiselle!"

Amanda shook her shriveled hand.

"Bonjour, Madame."

"You know, I've lived a long time. I've lived through two wars. I've had my times of doubts. I've known fights inside and outside, but I've learned something, and I'm going to tell you. This is the truth . . . ."

She pointed her finger toward the ceiling and whispered, as if telling a secret.

"He is faithful!"

LIFE AND DEATH

AMANDA WAS IN BED, ON HER cot. Next to her, Tante Mimi was already in deep sleep, but she could not sleep. She was known for liking food. However, she had barely touched her grandmother's dinner.

She was thoughtful and a little sad, too. She meditated on the words she had heard that morning.

Suddenly, quietly, and softly the light dawned in her spirit.

Jesus is alive!

She sat up and laughed for joy. She tried to spot Tante Mimi in the dark, and then she buried her face in her pillow, shaken with laughter. She did not want to wake her. When she fell asleep, angels rejoiced in heaven.

* * *

On Easter Monday, in the afternoon, the doorbell rang loudly. The Frey family was back. Mélissa and Amanda could barely wait to be together again—just the two of them. As soon as they were allowed to, they disappeared into Tante Mimi's bedroom. Amanda sat on her cot while Mélissa chose the desk chair.

"Mélissa, I have some great news for you," Amanda started right away.

"Wait a minute! It was my turn to talk."

"No way, my turn wasn't finished yet!" Amanda said, laughing.

"I believe Jesus is alive!"

Mélissa's eyes shone.

"This is wonderful!"

"And you know what? I'm so sure of it; if I were broken into little pieces, each piece would still believe it. I believe it as sure as you and I are alive!"

"Thank you, Lord!"

They looked at each other like two confederates.

"Well! Now, I'm going to confide in you!"

Mélissa got up, pushed the chair back, took a dance position, and started to hum a piece of music. She moved around lightly, graciously, and swiftly. Then, as suddenly as she had started, she stopped.

"I can't get on my toes; I don't have my dancing shoes," she explained.

She sat back.

"Amanda! My dance teacher wants to take me to the Opéra de Paris. Maman said yes. When I'm older, I'll be a dancer!"

Amanda observed her cousin, quietly. She was beautiful with her long, soft, brown hair falling freely on her shoulders.

"Actually . . ." Mélissa went on, "maybe not! There's something else I'd like to do with my life, maybe about as much."

"Just tell me!"

"This is very different," she prepared her cousin. "I would like to be a missionary."

"A missionary? What's that?"

"It's someone who brings the good news of God's salvation through Jesus Christ to those who haven't yet heard."

"Well . . . which one would you prefer?"

Mélissa thought for a while, wavering.

"I really don't know. It's still too early to tell. When I'm older, I'll be a dancer, or a missionary. What about you? What would you like to do later?"

"Oh . . . I don't know."

"You surely have some idea!"

Now, it was Amanda's turn to hesitate.

"I do, but I don't know how possible it could be."

"All the same, say it!"

"Well . . . if dreaming is allowed, I'd like to become a violinist." She said, laughing. "Just imagine, Mélissa! We'll meet each other at the Opéra de Paris. You'll dance and I'll play the violin."

Mélissa got up again and danced a few steps on the few square meters of the carpet, but she interrupted herself.

"Come on, Amanda, play some violin music for me."

Amanda pulled a box out from under the bed and got her violin out of its case. She carefully tuned it and played "What a Friend We Have in Jesus."

When the soft music stopped, Mélissa said, "You know what? Let's pray about that! We ought to trust God with all of our plans."

The two young ladies closed their eyes and bowed their heads.

* * *

It had been about a week since the Vissacs had come back from vacation. Amanda had just celebrated her thirteenth birthday. Now, she was back to school. On Monday afternoon, recess was coming to an end when the school director came up to her.

"Before you go to your class, would you please stop at my office?"

She stared at him. He was a little man: gentle, always serious. He looked concerned.

"Oui, Monsieur."

She had never been called up to his office before. As she walked toward it, she saw Jean-Baptiste was joining her.

"You, too?"

He nodded.

"I wonder what's wrong."

The director let them in and closed the door.

"Your mother just called. She asked me to inform you of a situation—to prepare you."

He swallowed some air.

"Your cousin, the daughter of her sister, just had a serious accident on the road. I can't tell you any more than that. Your mother will tell you when you get home."

The two children looked at each other. Jean-Baptiste had turned slightly pale. Amanda smiled weakly. It was impossible to concentrate during her last course.

* * *

When the children arrived at home, they stopped at their mother's bedroom entryway. She sat by the window, a Bible open on her lap, a handkerchief in one hand. Her eyes were red from crying. She stared through the window.

"Maman!" Amanda called, frozen to the ground.

"Dear children, Mélissa is dead."

Jean-Baptiste let out a cry of pain and fell on the bed, sobbing. Their mother hurried up and threw her arms around him. Amanda still had not moved. Tears silently ran down her cheeks.

* * *

At supper time, as the family sat around the table, Louise explained.

"Tomorrow, Papa and I are going back to Belfort. You'll have to stay on your own for three days. My sister needs me. I trust you. You're both old enough to take care of yourselves."

"Maman, I want to come."

"I know you do, Amanda, but we have just come back from there and our budget doesn't allow us to do more. I told Marguerite, Didi's mother. She'll keep an eye on you."

Her father added gently, "It's better to keep a memory of her alive."

"But she is alive," Amanda declared.

Armand stared at his daughter.

"She loved the Lord Jesus Christ. I'm sure she's with Him now," she explained.

"Why, you're absolutely right, Honey."

* * *

The next evening, when the children came back home from school, the house seemed sad and empty. They got busy straightening it up. Amanda washed the dishes. Jean-Baptiste swept the morning crumbs and cleaned up the table.

Once they were done with the chores, Amanda went into her room and sat comfortably on her bed. She took her mother's Bible, but did not open it right away.

She thought, *Lord, why did You take my cousin back? I mean . . . she wanted to serve You. She wanted to be a missionary!*

She waited, silently.

Alright, Lord, I belong to You now. You're my Lord and Master, but I'll never be as gentle and spiritual as my cousin. You know me! Are You sure You know what You are doing?

She sighed.

I don't have the slightest idea of how to become a missionary, but if this was on Your mind, Lord, I'm available. However, You'll have to show me all the way or forget about it!

She opened the Bible and continued reading where she had left off in the Evangile de Matthieu.

* * *

The children had left their entry door wide open to let the warmth of the day penetrate their cool house. The night was slowly settling in. Marguerite tiptoed in. She stopped in front of Amanda's open bedroom door.

"Coucou!"

She carried a hot pot from which came the delicious aroma of freshly made vegetable soup.

"What are you doing?" she asked.

"I'm reading the Bible."

"I don't believe that!" the dear lady muttered.

She had always claimed to be an atheist.

"I can't believe it!" she repeated.

Tears came up to her eyes. She went into the kitchen. Amanda got up.

"Marguerite, you shouldn't have! That's so kind of you. We would have gotten along."

"Well, then. I won't hear about that!"

Marguerite was a real mother hen. She hurried to set the table and served the hot soup to the children.

"This will do you good. One needs at least one warm meal a day."

She left them sitting at the table and disappeared as discreetly as she had come in.

* * *

The news of the loss that had just stricken the Vissac family rapidly spread throughout the whole village. Amanda was not able to join in the laughter and games of her schoolmates yet. Along with a new bus driver, the school district had acquired a new, modern school bus that sat people two-by-two. Every day, she looked for a seat to sit alone.

One evening, as she stared through the bus pane, Linda stepped in. They had not seen much of each other over the past year. The girl came up to her.

Linda asked shyly, "May I sit next to you?"

She glanced back at her.

"Well, sure!"

She removed her school bag from the free seat next to her. Linda sat down. They remained silent for a while, until the bus driver turned the engine on.

"I'm sorry for your cousin," Linda said, finally.

Amanda nodded.

"Thanks."

"Amanda, I would like to ask you something."

"Go ahead."

"I've been watching you for several days. I never saw you cry. How do you do that?"

Amanda turned away to avoid the stare of her friend.

"I'm afraid that my answer will cause you some grief."

"I am full of grief. Don't be afraid; you won't add to it. Just, I want to know."

Amanda looked back at her and sighed deeply.

"You see, my cousin loved the Lord Jesus Christ with all her heart. Her body is dead, but she's alive. She's with God. I'm sure of that. This is why I can't even cry."

Linda looked down.

"I don't know where my cousins are and I miss them terribly," she murmured.

"Still do?" her friend asked gently, adding, "I'm going to miss my cousin, too. She was one of my best friends."

Linda got up.

"Come on, Amanda, come with us. Don't isolate yourself."

"Not today, but maybe tomorrow. Thank you for caring."

They smiled at each other.

★ ★ ★

At the end of the school year, Amanda had reached an average mark of 17 out of 20. She had broken all of her previous records and the record of the three, seventh-grade sections altogether.

TELLING THE TRUTH

Thym, Octobre 1975
Chère Miriam,
I miss you very much. I feel so lonely since you moved, but I hope you are happy where you are and you have found some good friends.

This year, Linda is in my class again, but she does not dare to stay with me. She is from here, and it is not a good thing to be seen with me. I suppose I am too different. I understand her and I am not holding it against her.

Send me some news. Greet your family for me.

Your friend,
Amanda

★ ★ ★

IT WAS RECESS. THE STUDENTS PASSED through the English classroom to leave their schoolbags at their desks before going outside. The teacher, Mme Jolin, rewound a lesson tape and searched for the beginning of the next lesson. The classroom was about empty so she left the tape recorder there to go join her colleagues for the break.

Josie and Sophie hated the study of English. They ran to the door to make sure the teacher was out of sight, and then came back and drew close to the tape player.

"Leave this thing alone!"

"You mind your business!"

Amanda sighed. It was useless. Sophie began to push buttons in and out. The tape recorder played. She stopped it, rewound it, fast-forwarded it and finally rewound everything. Then, she opened the tape recorder and lifted the tape out of it. She pinched the strip and started to pull it out. Finally, the two girls abandoned it that way and ran outside, giggling.

Amanda considered the damage. Nothing was broken, but the tape . . . she did not dare touch it. Now, the classroom was empty. She slowly walked out.

★ ★ ★

When the whole class came back in, everybody noticed the tape right away. Then, the teacher entered. She stopped sharp.

"Who did that?"

A perfect silence answered her. It was obvious to her there were those who knew and those who did not know anything, but how to recognize them? She did not have much choice.

"If those who did this don't admit to it, I'm going to punish the whole class."

Groans could be heard.

"You'll have to write a two-page essay on the respect of public goods."

The protest became louder.

The teacher worked diligently to get the tape back into working order. She found the lesson she was looking for. They had lost fifteen minutes of work.

When the bell sounded at the end of the session, Mme Jolin gave her class a last chance.

"I'm asking for those who did this to come forward and tell me. That would be better for everyone."

Again, a perfect silence answered her. She sighed.

"Alright, for lack of better information, you'll all be punished."

The teenagers cleaned up their desks with murmurs of discontent. Amanda was irritated with herself because she was so slow. It seemed she was always the last one to clean out her desk.

She tried to throw her workbooks quickly in her bag, but there were still the pens. Nearly everybody else had departed and she still had one book left. Mme Jolin had finished putting her things in order. She waited, determined to lock the door this time.

There were still three students in the room. Finally, Amanda closed her bag. Mme Jolin turned to her.

"Amanda, would you know who touched the tape recorder?"

Taken aback, Amanda blushed. She opened her mouth but did not answer. Mme Jolin waited.

"Oui, Madame," she said finally.

The teacher's face brightened. She held onto a track.

"Well then, you can tell me who it is."

Amanda was hesitant.

"Non, Madame, I can't."

"Why can't you?"

"That would be tattling and it's bad!"

Mme Jolin thought quickly.

"To tell the truth is not tattling; not to tell the truth is taking part in the wrongdoing. Do you know that to help justice is a good citizen's duty?"

"I told you the truth," Amanda defended herself. "Concerning the names of the persons, it's up to them to reveal who they are."

The teacher was smart and she was not ready to give up. She decided to play the game.

"Well, then. I'll ask you the questions and you answer me. This way, it won't be tattling. It would be girls, right?"

Amanda sighed.

"Oui, Madame."

"This will reduce my choice by half. Would it be Yvette or Véronique?"

"Non, Madame."

"Would it be Sophie by any chance?"

Amanda felt trapped. She just could not make herself give the answer.

"Come on, tell me the truth; is it Sophie or not?" Mme Jolin insisted.

Amanda swallowed hard.

"Oui, Madame. She wasn't alone, either, but I'll let her tell you about that."

"Well, I thank you for that," Mme Jolin concluded, locking the door.

Gislaine and Maxime had been there through the entire conversation.

* * *

Lunchtime, with its two hours of recess, never seemed to come to an end. Amanda walked under the tall trees shading a meadow between the schoolyard and sports ground. She was bored and looked frequently at her watch. She could not wait to get back into class, but the time was not running any faster.

That day, she was coming out of the sports ground where the boys played soccer when she noticed Sophie, Josie, and Yvette in the far end of the courtyard, walking arm-in-arm. They laughed and seemed to be moving toward her. When they got within voice-reaching range, they called her.

"Come, we have something to show you!"

Amanda slowly started toward them. They moved faster to meet her, a welcoming smile on all their faces. Sophie, who walked in the middle, stopped right in front of her.

"We have an account to settle. I owe you something," she said.

A slap in the face surprised Amanda. However, she did not look down.

"Are you done?" she asked.

Taken aback, Sophie hesitated.

"Yes, I am."

The three girls turned around and moved away, laughing. Amanda looked around. There was nobody under the big trees, except Evelyne, a girl whom she had known since primary school. Evelyne was older than her, but had usually been kind to her. She walked up to Amanda.

"I saw everything," she simply said. "They're crazy. I don't like them."

They walked side-by-side, without talking anymore. Then, Amanda leaned against the biggest of the trees in an angle where she could not be seen by anyone else.

"Evelyne, may I trust you with something?"

"Sure!"

"You must promise you won't tell anybody."

"Why, I promise."

"I wish Miriam was still here," she sighed. "I feel so alone."

Tears filled her eyes. Evelyne stood by her quietly. Amanda quickly wiped her face with the back of her hand, and then bravely smiled.

"But I'll be alright. Thank you for stopping by."

Evelyne smiled back at her and left her to be with girls her age.

* * *

Soon after, at lunchtime, Amanda sat on the end of the bench at the school lunch-stall. Seven other girls sat with her at the table. Chantal was seated in front of her and Linda was at the other end.

A lady brought the dessert. It was individual, strawberry pies topped with whipped cream. Each girl took her share. Amanda was about to bite into her pie when Chantal, suddenly, pushed the pastry right into her face. The girls began to laugh. Amanda, her nose covered with cream, barely retrieved her pie, but the poor thing was so out of shape she decided to use it as a flying object and sent it right back into the face of the girl in front of her. Chantal saw it coming and ducked, just in time.

However, the pie splattered some of her long hair. She was upset. The other girls took her side right away.

"Honestly, you don't understand even a joke. She only wanted to have fun."

M. Gino slowly moved to the table. Amanda wiped her face while Chantal wiped her hair.

Amanda answered, quietly, "Yes, I do like jokes. I just wanted to have some fun, too. What are you complaining about? After all, it was my pie that was lost, not hers!"

"What's going on here?" asked the supervisor.

"It's her fault!" all the girls answered, unanimously, pointing to Amanda.

M. Gino looked at Amanda, severely.

"Do you really think I pushed my own pie in my face?" the girl protested.

"Look at her hair, sir!" Josie accused, pointing at Chantal.

The man scrutinized Amanda, frowning. He had seen her reaction.

Amanda shrugged.

"It was my pie. Lost for lost."

M. Gino sighed. He did not know what to make of it. He shrugged also, turned, and walked away.

"We won't talk to you anymore!" the girls told Amanda with disgusted looks on their faces.

* * *

That evening, as the young people got off the bus, Linda quickly walked away. Amanda called her.

"Hey, Linda, wait for me!"

As her friend did not answer, she ran after her, but Linda did not slow down. However, she caught up with her.

Amanda insisted, out of breath, "Come on Linda! Wait for me. We'll walk together."

Linda did not even look at her. Without a word, she went on her way as fast as possible.

Amanda slowed down. She got the message. Sadness overtook her. From that day on, Linda stopped talking to her for several months.

MOTUS ET BOUCHE COUSUE

ONE WEDNESDAY AFTERNOON, AMANDA READ, SITTING comfortably on her bed, when someone knocked at her door. She ran to open it.

"Salut, Didi!"

Didi, a ten-year-old girl, was four years younger than her.

"May I play with you?"

"I was waiting for you."

The young girl smiled. Amanda thought, for a few seconds, while trying to wrinkle her nose.

"Let me see . . . How about you helping me build a branch hut in the little woods that's behind here?"

"Sure, let's go!"

"It's about time we have a place of our own, far from eavesdroppers."

She covertly referred to imaginary spies, as she put on her coat.

Outside, the sun shined, but the air was cool. Her young friend was used to following her anywhere she would go so long as it was Wednesday. Amanda loved her. She was resourceful and good company.

They walked up a little street that passed by the village recreational hall and its chestnut trees, and arrived at the start of a dirt road that ran between the fields. Grass was growing down its middle. At the entrance of that path were an old farm, to the left, and a very old stone wall to the right.

Soon the landscape opened up into plowed fields. A lark sang high in the cloudless sky. The air was filled with the strong odor of snails after a rainy day. They hurried, impatient to arrive at the woods. In fact, it was more of an animal shelter in the middle of a land of soft clods.

As soon as they got there, they began to work. Three straight tree trunks would be the corners of the room. There were enough dead branches in that place to stack them up into walls and a roof. After two hours of intensive labor, the girls, green from the dust of the trees and covered with sweat, admired their construction.

Didi was already sitting inside the hut. She pulled a cookie box out of the backpack her mother had handed her on her way out.

"Come on, Amanda! We'll snack in our new house!"

Amanda joined her, bending down to pass between the branches of a tight opening.

"It feels so good to be at home!" she exclaimed.

She sat on a stump that made a wonderful piece of furniture. Didi's mouth was already full. She offered her cookies to Amanda, but this one grinned.

"No, thank you! I'm dead thirsty. I'm going to tell you a secret."

Didi's eyes opened wide. She shook her head affirmatively.

"Can you keep a secret? It has to remain just between the two of us, alright?"

"A' right!" she managed to answer.

Amanda took her time, enjoying every minute of it.

"Do you see the street we took to come to the dirt road?"

Didi shook her head again.

"The name of that road is: Street of the Old Castle. I bet there was a castle there in the past. If there was a castle, there certainly was an underground passage, and if there was an underground passage, there could be a treasure."

Didi's eyes shone in the dark. She had finally emptied her mouth.

"A treasure? How cool! If we become rich, we'll be able to buy all the chestnut butter we want."

Amanda gave her a hard look.

"I hope you don't steal money from your mother anymore. You know I don't agree with that!"

"Don't worry, I didn't. She gave me the cookies, but I prefer chestnut butter."

"Good," Amanda sighed.

She started again, "I have a plan."

"What are we going to do?"

"First of all, we're going to explore the surroundings."

"Right!"

"Next . . . I've got an idea. I'm going to tell you what. At school, in civic instruction class, the teacher asked us to write a paper. We have to do some research on the origin of our village. I'm going to take advantage of that to go to the Town Hall. With that pretext, I'll look for some information about our castle."

Amanda realized she had lost Didi somewhere during the first sentence.

"Alright, I'll go to the Town Hall by myself and let you know what I have found."

"And what do I do?"

"You'll come to see me as soon as I send you word. I'll send you a secret message."

"Yes, like you showed me, with one letter, out of two, being the right one. Great! Let's go to explore right now!"

The girls started on their way back. They passed by the old wall when Didi stopped.

"Wait for me a minute. I want to have a closer look at that wall. Maybe there is a secret passage in it."

She followed the wall closely, her nose right on the stones. Suddenly, she called, excited.

"Amanda, come quick!"

Her big friend drew closer.

"Look at that!"

On one of the old stones, they could clearly see the carved shape of a heart, through which ran an arrow.

"Hmm . . . ," Amanda muttered, "I wonder how old this can be! This could be a remainder of our castle. Actually, this is the only ancient-looking piece I know of on this road."

They kept on going. Amanda was increasingly convinced if there had been a castle it had been where Didi's discovery confirmed it. She walked Didi to her home next to the church and the Town Hall; they said good-bye.

"Motus et bouche cousue!"[29]

"Motus et bouche cousue!"

That was their password. Amanda could not wait to go to the Town Hall. At its entrance, a few men talked. She greeted them, drew in her breath, and went in. She went up to the secretary's desk.

"Good afternoon, Madame."

"Good afternoon! What would you like, young lady?"

"I'm doing some research on the history of the village for a school paper. Would you have any information about it?"

"You know, this is a small village. There isn't much about it. Now that I remember, I might have something for you. Another young lady did the same type of research recently, except she did it for superior studies. She's with a college of agriculture. She left a copy of her findings with us. Let me see if I can find it."

She got up and went to look for it. Amanda hoped, with all her heart, she still had it. The kind lady opened a closet and drew a dossier out of it. She pulled forth a double sheet of paper, covered with a thin handwriting.

"Here it is. Look at that!"

---

29 "Cross my heart!"

Amanda took the document and started to decipher it. She looked up.

"This is exactly what I want. I would like to copy it. May I take it to my home? I'll bring it back as soon as I am done."

"Of course you may!" the secretary said, smiling at the young lady's visible excitement.

Amanda ran back home. She began to work right away, and then she wrote a little note:

DLISDEIVCDOMMSEDADSESSOQOUNEATSUYPOEUUCXARN

(Translated: Didi, come as soon as you can).

She slid the note into an envelope. The next morning, she would make a slight detour to put it in Didi's mailbox before she got on the school bus.

* * *

The next day, Didi arrived at 5:30 p.m., out of breath.

"Hi! I can't stay long. My mother is expecting me back at six. Tell me what you found!"

"Come in; hurry! I'm going to read what I brought back from the Town Hall. It's so exciting!"

Amanda sat at her desk while Didi got comfortable on her bed. She opened a drawer and pulled out the precious document she had copied, entirely by hand. She had added to it a map of the village she had found on a post office calendar.

She started to read: "The History of Thym: The Castle."

"The vaults of the cave have been preserved. In the back, one can see a kind of opening, totally obstructed with stones. Could it be the entrance to a secret passage? It would go to the ancient chapel destroyed a long time ago, passing by the Marquis.

"The *preaching square* is the garden behind the farmhouse. It's bordered on its other side by a large trench. Human bones have been found there, for this place would have been a protestant cemetery.

"On the back of the castle, bordered by a dirt road, one can still see a stone on which a heart, pierced by a sword, is engraved."

Didi, eyes shining, let out a shout.

"This is our stone!"

Amanda smiled, widely. She went on.

"The traces left of a monastery and a protestant cemetery seemed to indicate originally, a protestant office was practiced there."

The teenage girl interrupted herself.

"Didi! Do you realize there were Protestants here?"

Didi's eyes opened round.

"What are Protestants?"

"I don't know, exactly. They aren't Catholics. It's kind of like my grandfather, but you don't know my grandfather."

She thought for a minute.

"This is so curious. I wonder if their community would have been a little bit like in the book of Acts. Now, why would there be none left anymore?"

"Keep reading!"

Didi was becoming impatient.

"Alright, I'll pass over some details you wouldn't care for. It's a little bit complicated. Now, listen to this! A certain man, Didon, living on the farm, emigrated in 1810 and never came back. It's said he left behind a hidden treasure, but nobody ever found it. On the other hand, he might have taken it with him."

"If nobody ever found it, it might still be here!" Didi exclaimed.

"I doubt it. It rather seems, to me, if other people have searched for it before us, it might not be here any longer. Besides, if I had been that man, I would have taken my treasure with me. It's probably safer to find another way to get lots of chestnut butter," she teased her friend.

Didi laughed.

"What we've discovered is fascinating, but I've got to go. Maman is going to wait for me."

"D'accord. Motus et bouche cousue!"

"Motus et bouche cousue!"

The young girl went away, skipping about.

THE CALL OF THE SIREN

SPRINGTIME HAD COME BACK. ON ONE warm afternoon, the eighth graders of Amanda's class had difficulty concentrating on the natural sciences course that took place during the last hour of the day. Suddenly, through the wide-open windows, the sound of the town firehouse's siren came in, screaming.

Linda sat at the center of the class.

"Stop your circus antics!" Chantal exclaimed as she observed her.

Amanda, who sat on the front, turned around. Linda was pale and shaking all over. The teenagers surrounded her noisily. The teacher was losing control over the class.

"What's wrong with her?" he asked.

"She's crazy."

"No, she thinks she's at the theater."

"She's acting."

Linda's eyes filled with tears.

"What's the matter with you?" the teacher asked again.

"I don't know," Linda stammered. "When the siren sounded, it seemed like . . . like—"

Mocking laughs broke out. She was unable to finish her sentence. She swallowed back her tears. The teacher did not understand anything. Amanda bit her lip; she understood.

What to do?

"Everyone back to his place!" the teacher ordered.

Linda made a major effort to control herself, but her teeth quivered. When the session ended, the classroom was in a state of anarchy. As soon as the bell rang, the whole class surrounded the girl and sarcasm started to fly from all directions.

Linda had always been a very pretty girl and it seemed most of the girls strived for her friendship. Misguided, her classmates believed their sharp comments would force Linda to regain self-control. However, Amanda suspected some were jealous of her.

Led by the girls, the boys got into the game as well. Amanda, sickened, tried to get out of the room as fast as possible. However, the whole crowd followed her, in an uproar, dragging in their midst Linda, who still trembled.

"How impressive!"

"You're a great actress!"

It was too much. Amanda clenched her fists, turned around and faced the pack.

"Is that the way you're treating a friend?" she challenged them.

Just as she did, M. Gino, the supervisor, came behind them. She looked at him, relieved. He glanced back at her and quickly got an impression of the situation.

The group stopped and turned around. They became silent as the man passed slowly through their midst, without a word. He was competent and respected. However, as he did not know what was going on, he did not linger there. The fact that the students had calmed down was sufficient for him, so he disappeared into the teachers' room.

As soon as the pack went outside, it went wild again. Suddenly, Linda started to scream at the top of her voice. Surprised, the teenagers moved back.

Amanda took advantage of the situation to get close to her. She grabbed her by the shoulders, dragged her outside of the circle to a corner of the school building where she isolated her, and put a protective arm around her.

"It's okay, Linda," she gently said. "You can cry; it's good for you."

Slowly, the girl calmed down; her pain turned into tears that finally found their way down her cheeks. Now, the boys kept a respectful distance, but a group of loud girls was approaching, led by Josie and Chantal.

Amanda, worried, glanced behind her back. Instinctively, she opened the collar of her shirt.

"It's going to be hell here. We'd better get moving."

Linda did not seem to hear her. She did not show any sign of moving. She sobbed softly, lost in her own world, and they still had to go around the whole building.

"Come on, let's get to the bus as fast as possible," Amanda urged her.

She grabbed her arm and led Linda away. She did not offer any resistance. Meanwhile, as they reached the other side of the building, the girls caught up with them.

They grabbed hold of Linda's other arm. Amanda did not want to pull on the poor girl; she was forced to let go of her.

"Leave her alone!" they shouted at her. "She's not your friend."

"We'll take care of her."

"This is not your business."

They formed a thick wall between the two girls. Linda began to scream again with a piercing voice. Amanda, desperate, looked about. She spotted Aurélie on the outside of the group. She walked up to her.

"Aurélie, run to the teacher's room and get Monsieur Gino!" she whispered.

Aurélie looked at the group. She was hesitant. Amanda noticed Ginette, the daughter of the bus driver, had followed her and moved closer to them.

"Ginette, would you go with Aurélie to get Monsieur Gino?" Amanda begged in a low voice. "It's urgent."

Ginette nodded affirmatively.

"What if they try to keep us from it?"

"Take the forbidden entrance, it's the opposite way. They won't expect you to go that way and it's much faster."

"What if a teacher tries to stop us?"

"Just say I sent you."

The two girls left, running. The forbidden entrance led from this outside courtyard to the teachers' room. Nobody was in the way. They entered it.

Meanwhile, the teenage girls escalated into a state of panic. The commotion provided a space that allowed Amanda to get back to Linda. She took hold of her, pushed her against the wall of the building, and tried to protect her with her body.

"Don't worry; I'm not going to leave you!"

Linda could not hear anything.

Chantal and Josie still tried to separate them.

"Get out of here!"

"Come on, get lost!"

"You have nothing to do with us!"

Chantal grabbed Amanda's shirt at the shoulder and tried to pull her back, but this time Amanda struggled to resist.

"Get your hands off me!" she cried.

"Mind your business, stupid!" Chantal shouted back.

Suddenly, the grasp let go of Amanda. A strong grip jerked her assailant back. M. Gino's voice thundered.

"You're the stupid ones! Get out of here! Go! Right now!"

Gently, but firmly, he took the screaming girl from Amanda's arms and led her away, out of sight. The schoolgirls, ill at ease, scattered away promptly, like a flight of birds caught in fault. Only Aurélie and Ginette were still there, proud of the mission they had accomplished.

Amanda leaned against the wall. Her legs barely carried her. She trembled all over. She made an effort to smile at them.

"Thank you, girls!"

They smiled back and headed for the bus together. There was no hurry as they would have to wait for their friend. Instead, the director showed up.

"Linda won't take the bus tonight. Monsieur Gino will drive her home. It's on his way."

* * *

In Thym, when Amanda got off the bus, she noticed Linda's younger brother, who was coming back from school. He looked at the departing bus with a perplexed look on his face. She went up to him.

"Don't worry; your sister will arrive soon. She just wasn't feeling well and the supervisor is going to bring her back."

The boy nodded.

As she slowly walked home, following the main street, the sound of a car's engine got closer. She stepped out of the road onto the grassy slope. The blast of a horn made her jump. She turned around. At the wheel, M. Gino had slowed down.

With a wide smile spread on his face, he waved to her. Surprised, Amanda only waved back once his gray 2CV gained speed again. The car disappeared at the bend in the road.

Amanda sighed with contentment. M. Gino was happy with her, and Linda was probably back home—safe and sound. Most of all, for the first time in her life, she had a strong feeling of accomplishment.

* * *

The next morning, after breakfast, Amanda quickly washed her face and brushed her hair. Her parents had just gone off to work and Jean-Baptiste had already left the house. She still had to prepare her schoolbag and put her shoes on when someone knocked at the door. She frowned. It was not a time for a visit.

She opened the door wide and found herself face-to-face with Linda. She could not hide her surprise.

"Ah . . . hi!"

Linda peacefully observed her.

"I came to thank you for yesterday."

"Oh . . . No problem."

"I don't know what happened to me," she tried to explain.

Amanda hesitated, and then said gently, "Do you think the sound of the siren reminded you of your cousins?"

Stunned, Linda did not answer right away.

"You might be right!"

After a silence, she looked Amanda straight in the eyes.

"I also want to ask for forgiveness for ignoring you these past months."

Taken aback, Amanda did not answer.

"Will you please forgive me?" the young lady insisted, with sadness.

"Sure, I will! You've always been my friend," she finally answered, with all her heart.

"Well . . . thanks! See you at the bus then!"

She was about to turn back when Amanda stopped her.

"Wait a minute. Could we walk to the bus together?"

"Are you ready?"

"No, but please, wait for me. It'll take two minutes."

Linda waited politely outside while Amanda, seized by a feverish joy, threw her books into her bag at an amazing speed. Her shoelaces were half-tied when she stepped outside.

She turned the key in the lock and slid it under a stone. Everybody knew the hiding place, but it was just for the form.

"Let's go!"

It was a beautiful spring day. The honeysuckle along the way bloomed and its sweet fragrance filled the air. The birds were singing. Amanda laughed and chattered while Linda listened to and watched this strange friend. She smiled quietly.

"Amanda!"

"Oui?"

"How about you finish tying your shoelaces!"

THE PRIEST'S DAUGHTER

THE FALL OF 1976 WAS ALREADY well-advanced, as the beginning of the new school year was several weeks earlier. One of the two ninth-grade classrooms had been arranged to be a one-room building apart from the big school buildings. It was aptly called: the Prefab.

Its wood-board floor resounded under the feet of the teenagers. On rainy days the roof, made of iron sheets, echoed the thousands of raindrops in a loud and continual roll.

Amanda found this environment friendlier than the other classrooms. She had chosen her desk at the back of the room. Linda was on her right-hand side, against the wall. The other girls systematically refused to occupy the seat on her left-hand side. Two boys had already been there.

On Friday afternoon, the class had one hour of study. Sometimes the young people took the opportunity to exchange seats before the supervisor came.

Etienne Langio was a good student. He approached the front seats.

"Joël, would you exchange your place with mine? I'd like to get closer to the front."

"Are you in your right mind? Just get lost!"

Etienne sighed. He tried the girl at the next desk.

"Please, would you like to swap seats with me? I'm right in the middle."

"Don't even dream about it. Go get stuck somewhere else." Aurélie answered before Etienne even asked.

"No way! I'm keeping my place. I need to be at the front to work well."

Etienne decided to give the second row a try. Chantal stood up.

She shouted with a shrill voice, "Look everybody! Don't you think he looks like an Ay-rab?"

All the heads turned to gaze at his black curly hair. Laughs started to burst out.

"Yes, that's right, he does!"

"He's an 'Ay-rab!'"

"Hey 'Ay-rab!' What do you want?"

Etienne, standing in the middle of the aisle, passed a hand through his thick hair.

"I'm of Italian descent!" he protested.

"You liar! Everybody knows the Arabs came to Sicily. There must be some Arabs among your ancestors," Josie accused.

"Yep! You're ashamed of it, right?"

Part of the class started to sing together, "Ay-rab! Ay-rab!"

The boy, embarrassed, tried to return to his seat, but Chantal obstructed his way.

"Look, everybody; see what an Ay-rab looks like!"

Amanda got up, "Leave him alone! He's not an Arab—and even if he was, there's no shame in it!"

The laughs calmed down. Chantal shrugged.

"This girl. What a party-pooper!"

Etienne's face relaxed. He walked slowly back up the aisle, forcing his way through desks and teenagers still trying to hold him back. He finally arrived at the back of the class and spoke to Amanda's left-hand neighbor.

"I'll exchange a well-situated spot, right in the middle of the classroom, for your desk."

The boy hesitated, surprised.

"Well . . . Alright!"

Without waiting any longer, he began to pick up his belongings and emptied his desk. Soon, Etienne, radiant, had settled into his new residence. He winked at Amanda.

"Oh no!" she moaned, sulking while sinking into her chair.

"Don't worry, I won't bother you!" he promised. "Only . . . could you pass me your eraser?"

She handed him her eraser.

"You'd better buy one as fast as possible!"

Etienne took the eraser and smiled, mysteriously.

"I do intend to never buy any," he answered audaciously.

Amanda, dismayed, looked down on her homework, determined to ignore him.

* * *

During one recess, Chantal, Josie, Nicole, and the other girls gathered together. As Amanda wandered by the group, Josie signaled for the girls to be quiet.

"Go away, you!" she told Amanda. "You're too young to listen to what we're saying."

"Well, good for me!" she answered without blinking. "I'd rather not hear what you say!"

She walked away without regret. After a while, Aurélie and Ginette left the group and came up to her. Ginette grinned.

"They're getting dirty. It's upsetting. My father wouldn't want me to mix with the wrong crowd."

"You're lucky," Aurélie remarked. "Your father is the bus driver and they're leaving you alone because they see him every day."

"Your mother wouldn't like this, either," Amanda noted.

"My mother teaches catechism," Aurélie explained to Ginette.

"It seems Nicole got pregnant and that she's already had an

abortion," Ginette whispered.

Amanda shivered.

"For sure, my mother wouldn't approve of that type of company." Aurélie recognized.

"What keeps you, then, from staying away from them?" Amanda asked her.

Aurélie dropped her voice:

"They want to run everything. Nicole claims she's the leader and maintains we must do all she orders. She wants each of the girls to have a boyfriend and kiss him."

"So what? Do you feel like kissing a boy?"

Aurélie blushed and wavered.

"There's one boy, whom I really like, but he doesn't even look at me—and I'm not interested in any other!"

"If I understand you correctly, you wouldn't kiss just anyone."

"Of course, not! I'd hate that!"

"Then, why would you agree to all of Nicole's whims and wishes?"

"Well . . . you know them . . . I think I'm scared of them," the teenager admitted.

"Oui!" Ginette agreed. "When they're together, they can be real nasty."

Amanda leaned against the wall of the covered school yard. She thought, quietly, for a minute. Aurélie had always been a year younger than the rest of the class, and Amanda had an instinct of protection toward her.

"Alright!" she finally said. "As far as I'm concerned, I'm not afraid of them. I know it's not fitting to be seen together, even now, but if you want to stick with me, I'll do whatever I can to protect you."

The girls were hesitant.

"Alright, I realize this is not a guarantee," Amanda acknowledged. "However, you must have courage in what you believe and, in any case, I won't let you down."

The two girls smiled, encouraged.

"We'll see what comes up, but thanks all the same!"

* * *

One week later, on Friday afternoon, the director came to the Prefab at the beginning of study time and entered the room.

"I'm short of supervisors today," he announced. "You're the oldest group here. Monsieur Gino will keep an eye on you as much as possible, but I trust you to behave yourselves and use your time to work well."

He stayed with the students until every single one of them had drawn out some homework. Then he left behind a silent and hardworking class.

As soon as he was far enough away, Nicole got up. She stared through the window. The director entered the main school building. She remained standing and started to count aloud the number of girls and the number of boys.

"Who is the boys' leader?" she asked.

The boys quickly came to an agreement.

"Thierry's fine."

Thierry was taller than the other boys by about a head. He smiled complacently.

"Alright!" Nicole went on. "There's about the same number of girls as boys. Therefore, each one of us can choose a boyfriend or a girlfriend."

"Yeah, yeah! Good idea!" Thierry approved.

"Come on everyone, chose a partner!" Nicole ordered.

Amanda sighed. It was becoming difficult for her to concentrate on a complicated math problem.

Nicole began to stroll along the rows and stopped at each desk to make sure her plan was being carried out. Chantal and Josie jumped up and down with excitement.

"I'll choose André. No, he's too short for me."

"Francis is more handsome." Josie went on, making eyes at the boy, who sat up.

Nicole had arrived at Aurélie's desk.

"So, have you chosen anyone yet?"

Aurélie grinned.

"I have, but he doesn't want me, so forget about it."

"Choose someone else, then!"

"Amanda says I don't have to."

"I hope you're not listening to that idiot!"

At the mention of Amanda's name, the brouhaha calmed down. Though seated at the back of the room and working on her math problem, she had an ear out and had not missed a word of what was being said. Ginette, who sat next to Aurélie, came to her rescue.

"And what if we don't feel like having a boyfriend?"

"I'm the leader and I decide. You've got to do as I say."

"And what if we refuse?"

"I'll force you! I'll slap you right across your ugly face!"

"Amanda says you can't force her," Aurélie retorted.

"And if you can't force her, then you're not the leader," Ginette provoked.

Nicole blushed with anger.

She shouted, "She's the daughter of a priest! That's what she is, and we're going to see who the leader in this class is."

She left the front row and stomped toward the back of the classroom. She shoved aside any obstacle that might slow her down, including students standing up.

"Come on, get out of my way!" she commanded. "I'm going to massacre the face of that Christian."

Little-by-little, the teenagers began sitting down, pulling chairs and bags aside to clear the way.

"Hey, the Christian!" some smirked.

"Chantal!" Nicole ordered. "Keep an eye out at the window! Make sure you warn me if anyone shows up!"

Chantal took her post by the window. Josie joined her to keep her company.

Though Nicole was about half way through, Amanda had not yet looked up.

"Amanda Vissac, I'm talking to you!"

Amanda straightened. She saw Nicole step over a bag and move toward her with a sudden calm that appeared dangerous. Carefully, Amanda closed her workbook and put her pen down. The room became amazingly silent.

"Go ahead! I'm listening to you. What do you want?"

Nicole slowed down and stopped a couple of steps from her.

"In this class, I'm the leader!" she declared. "Even the boys have a leader and nobody disagrees. You're the only one who never wants to do like everyone else, so I'm going to force you to submit."

This speech was welcomed by groans of approval. Amanda was not in a hurry. She calmly crossed her arms in front of her. She did not glance away from the hard, long look of the girl.

"Just tell me. Who *said* you were the leader?"

"Everybody agrees!"

"Sorry, but I don't!"

"Maybe, but you have to accept the majority!"

"To start with, nobody ever asked me for my opinion; second, you're not a leader. You're a dictator!"

Nicole moved swiftly and raised her hand.

"I'm going to destroy your face!" she shouted.

Amanda clenched her teeth as the girl was right in front of her.

Behind her, the door flew open and M. Gino erupted into the classroom. As fast as lightning, the attacker put her arm down and walked to her place as if nothing had happened.

"What are you doing here, you?" the supervisor asked Nicole severely.

Amanda breathed. M. Gino went around the room, slowed down by her desk, glanced at her, and left as he had arrived. It seemed obvious he had been listening behind the door for a while. The teenagers went quietly back to work.

VIOLINIST

AMANDA'S NINTH GRADE CLASS WAS NOW less than three months away from the examination of the Brevet des Collèges. As French class was over, Amanda got up and walked to the teacher's desk.

The French teacher was responsible for the administrative matters of her class. He was also the music teacher. She handed him a letter from her parents, which he opened.

"Well! It looks like you're going to play the violin in Germany."

"Yes, I'm part of the orchestra that accompanies a choir."

"How come you're going to Germany?"

"It's because of the twin towns," she explained. "La Serpe is the twin town of Bergen in Germany. They have invited us to celebrate the union; I think I'll be the youngest on that trip."

"So, you're leaving in two days."

"Yes, and I'll have to miss school for a couple of days, if it's alright with you."

"I think it's great. Tell me, Amanda, would you be willing to bring your violin to class once and play something for us?"

She smiled.

"I sure would, but not before I come back!"

* * *

The town of La Serpe had reserved a whole train to go to Germany. Amanda, the junior of the trip, had been entrusted to the care of the orchestra. She hardly slept that night, sitting between a flutist and violinist. At their arrival in the morning, welcoming families waited for them.

She was so tired she did not remember how she arrived at her abode. A young woman, very kind, showed her a neat little bedroom. She sunk into a soft comforter and lost all consciousness of time.

When she woke up, she smiled.

I'm in Germany!

She washed up quickly, got dressed, and stepped out of her bedroom to go on a discovery trip. She descended some stairs and followed the sound of voices. Thus, she arrived at the kitchen.

"Guten tag!" she said.

Frau Werner turned around, smiling.

"Guten abend!"

It was already the evening. The hostess pointed to a young girl sitting at the table.

"Das ist Nikol!"

"Guten abend, Nikol."

The little one greeted her with a large smile. Amanda understood right away that none of them spoke French. She then realized her own knowledge of the German language was very limited.

They tried to communicate through sign language. Frau Werner tried to speak English. The three ladies were having a good time, laughing, when Herr Werner came in.

"Das ist Franz!" Frau Werner introduced him.

"Bonjour!" said the young man. "How are you doing?"

"You speak French!" exclaimed Amanda, relieved.

"Yes, I do! I hope you had a good rest. We're very honored to receive you at our home. If you need anything, just let us know."

"Thank you, very much; this is very kind of you. I have a present for you from my parents."

She ran back to her room to get a porcelain dish her mother had chosen, especially for them.

After they had admired the gift, Franz started again, with his heavy German accent, "How old are you?"

"I'll be fifteen soon."

"You're still very young. Nikol, my daughter, is eight years old."

"She's lovely."

"Thank you. Tomorrow is Saturday. It's the big celebration day. What are you going to play?"

"We shall play a cantata of Bach."

"Of course, Bach is beautiful!" he approved.

* * *

During the celebration, Amanda joined her orchestra. She played with the second violins. When the concert was over, she looked for her German family. They were proud to have with them one of the youngest musicians. They stopped with her and Nikol for ice cream.

* * *

The next day, the whole family slept in.

After a late breakfast, Franz proposed, "Today is Sunday. It's already your last day here. We'll spend it as a family. We would like to go out and show you some of the German countryside. How would you like that?"

"This is a great idea! I love the countryside! I, myself, come right from there."

"Gut!"[30]

Franz seemed to be hesitant.

---

30 German word for: good

He added, "I would like also to talk to you . . . if you don't mind."

Amanda observed the young father's face and looked straight into the sharp eyes.

"I don't see why not," she agreed. "Anytime!"

"Later, during our outing!" he answered, mysteriously.

Franz Werner got the whole family into his car. They drove out of town and came to a wooded area blossoming in spring colors. After they got out of the car, Frau Werner and Nikol took out a Frisbee and invited Amanda to join them in their play, but she preferred to watch them.

She sat on the grassy slope, under the light shade of the young leaves hardly starting to bud. The man was about to join them, but his wife talked to him. Amanda understood she asked him to keep her company.

"Ya, ya," he said.

He came to sit next to her and they watched the players run and jump after the plastic disk, laughing. After a while, they started to pursue each other and disappeared into the woods.

"Well," Franz said. "Everything is quiet now. It would be a good time to talk. What do you think?"

He was serious and a little bit tense.

"Alright! Go ahead!"

He breathed deeply, looking away, his sight lost on the farmlands.

He began, softly, "In the name of my country, and in the name of my family, I would like to ask you for forgiveness for the German aggression on France."

Amanda lost her voice. He lightly turned towards her.

"Well," she finally answered awkwardly. "You know, I wasn't born yet."

He sighed.

"Neither was I."

She gazed at him. He looked like he was not yet thirty years old, but there was sadness in his eyes. He did not give up.

"Did your family suffer from that war?"

Amanda thought for a while.

"During the First World War, my grandmother, on my father's side, lost her fiancé. Later, she married my grandfather, who was also her cousin. As far as I know, nobody died in their family.

"In 1916, my grandfather was a taxi driver. He was requisitioned to bring supply to the troops. At one point, as he was out talking with three other drivers, he left the group to go get something in his vehicle. As he moved away, a bomb exploded in the middle of his friends, killing all of them. My grandfather was wounded by shrapnel, but he lived."

Franz respected a silence, and then began, again, with clenched teeth.

"How about the Second World War?"

"My parents remember they were hungry. My father was sixteen then. His parents sent him to live with their family in the mountains in Haute-Loire. There, he ate, alright."

"What about your mother?"

"My mother lived in Alsace. Her parents and grandparents lost all their possessions during that time. Of course, they never recovered them."

"Alsace!"

The German slowly helped her to become conscious of her past.

"Was anyone killed in your family?"

"My grandfather had to hide in order to not go to work in the German factories, but he survived."

The man waited a little bit.

"Is that all?"

She hesitated.

"My grandmother lost her younger brother, Emile. He was killed during the war, in the Black Forest. He was my mother's godfather. I heard he was very kind."

Herr Werner looked down. He prayed again, softly.

"Would you please forgive us, in the name of your family?"

This time, Amanda knew what to do.

"Yes," she answered without any hesitation. "I will!"

His face relaxed with a light smile. His wife and daughter ran in the sun.

"Thank you," he said. "And never forget it when you go back to your country!"

"I won't forget you Franz Werner, nor your family," she promised. "And I'll let my parents know about what happened between us."

He held his hand out to her. She shook it as the symbol of their alliance.

* * *

After her return from Germany, Amanda brought her violin to school, as promised. All her schoolmates gathered around her and her violin case.

"Open it, please, open it!" Chantal begged.

Amanda could not help, but smile at all the energy this girl had.

"Sorry, old friend, but you're far too excited. If something happened to this violin you couldn't replace it. I'm going to leave it in the teachers' room and you can see it when I take it out to play."

The girls had learned not to argue with Amanda. They waited impatiently for the French class. When finally the teacher gave his consent, Amanda drew the precious instrument out of its case and displayed it to her schoolmates who listened to her very attentively.

"I'm going to play for you the first movement of a Vivaldi concerto," the young musician announced.

The silence was impressive. Amanda tucked her instrument under her chin and opened with the joyous allegro of the great Italian composer. When she stopped, the eyes of all of her comrades shined.

"Would you like more?" she asked.

"Please!" they answered unanimously.

However, the teacher refused.

"I'm sorry, but unfortunately we're preparing for the brevet. It's an important examination and we can't afford any more entertainment. However, maybe another time . . . ."

His decision was not welcomed, but Amanda put her instrument away.

* * *

At recess, boys and girls surrounded her.

"It was wonderful," Josie said.

"I don't think I've ever heard anything so beautiful," Chantal declared whole-heartedly. "You know what? We're organizing a party for the end of the school year on behalf of the two ninth-grade classes. We would like you to attend."

Amanda laughed.

"You're sure? I'm afraid you'll be disappointed. I'm a musician alright, but I'm not a dancer."

"Oh yes, you come!" Etienne Langio insisted. "You'd better come. I've been waiting for this time since the beginning of the school year."

Instead of answering, she grinned at him.

* * *

The math and German teachers had agreed to supervise the party, which was being held in a classroom. The students had pushed the desks against the walls and arranged the chairs in a circle. A tape recorder alternated between slow pop-music and rock-and-roll tunes, one after the other. That was about all the teenagers knew at that time.

Amanda did not want to disappoint them, so she was there, but she had found a comfortable place in a corner. She did not intend to move away from it. She watched her school friends swaying with the music of her time.

Between each piece, the teenagers changed partners. Several boys tried to bring her into the dance, but so far she had managed to turn them away.

"I promise you I dance like a hippopotamus on dry ground. You'll be horribly ashamed with me."

Etienne was rock-and-rolling all by himself when a slower dance started. He began to come up to the young lady, without haste, sure of himself. She shook her head vigorously, negatively.

He stopped, a step away from her, and bent one knee to the ground. In a style that would have made a Middle Ages knight envious, he held his hand out to her.

He asked, "Mademoiselle, voulez-vous danser avec moi?"[31]

Amanda started to laugh. It seemed to her everybody watched them. The teenagers had wide smiles on their faces. She could not possibly refuse him; it would be a true public disgrace. She got up.

"You're looking for trouble. You might regret it!" she warned.

Without a word, the boy led her leisurely around the dance floor.

"This is not a dance," she remarked. "We're just walking in circles."

"We can try rocking together if you prefer."

"Mercy! That would be worse. We'd look like ducks waddling."

She started to laugh uncontrollably. Etienne, imperturbable, led his girl in the rhythmical steps.

At the end of their dance, however, he admitted, disgusted, "Really, you're impossible to dance with!"

He had barely let go of her when Philippe, whom she had barely seen since seventh grade, took hold of her. The tape played another popular tune. She made an effort to calm down. The math teacher

---

31 "Milady, would you dance with me?"

waltzed with the German teacher. He passed by the two teenagers.

"Hey, Philippe! Proud to dance with the violinist?" he called.

Philippe was kind and quiet, but Amanda could not wait to finish that dance. As soon as it was over, she rushed outside and found Aurélie and Ginette who tried to cool off.

"Ouf!" she exclaimed. "I'm not going back in there!"

Aurélie shook her head.

"You're so bizarre! I'd love to have all those boys coming after me."

"Don't say so," Amanda protested. "They're sweet, but I don't wish to give them any false hope!"

EPILOGUE

MY BROTHER, JEAN-BAPTISTE, LEFT THE VILLAGE of Thym at the age of sixteen to start on a Tour de France with the Compagnons du Devoir. In 1983, he was received as Companion Carpenter in Paris. He was named, according to the tradition, after the region which he came from: Jean-Baptiste le Beauceron, even though he had always been kind of a stranger there and he never went back there to live.

* * *

It was several years before I found out the Protestants of that region had once made up nearly 40 percent of the population before being wiped out through persecution.

* * *

Thirty years later, on the occasion of a ninth-grade class reunion, I took my American husband to visit the village of Thym where I had grown up and where I had left around that time. I was anxious to arrive there as speedily as possible. I was fearful my little school would not be there anymore—ravaged, perhaps, by time.

When we stopped at the edge of the village, everything seemed intact, only a little run-down. My husband entered the schoolyard.

Soon, someone talked to him. I drew closer. A little lady with white hair had opened the window of her house, like in the old times.

I shouted, "Madame Roussette!"

She looked at me and pronounced my name, "Amanda Vissac." Then she slowly wondered aloud, "But . . . but how did I remember that name, after thirty years?"

She hurried out of her home and came to us.

"Yes, I know why I remember. You were different, always respectful of others."

I nudged my husband in his side.

"Pay attention to what she says!"

My husband was pleased to take a picture of me with my first grade schoolteacher. The one I used to look up to from below was now much shorter than I. She allowed me to put my arm around her shoulders.

When we attended the only class reunion I ever had, I found my ninth-grade schoolmates had hardly changed; they were simply a little older. I was saddened to learn only a handful was still married to the spouse of his or her youth.

I realized how much I had loved them. At school, we had been taught academic subjects, but not the basics of life.

COMING FALL 2014:
THE SONG OF THE VIOLA

THE STORY OF AMANDA IS TRUE. Would you like to know more about her life? After moving again . . .

★ ★ ★

After moving again, the Vissac family settles in the town of La Serpe. There, Amanda enters high school and finds herself confronted with the haunting questions of youth. What career should she choose? What boy can she go out with? What saint can she trust?

Her only certainty was her faith, undeniably, added some spice to her life!

For more information about
AMANDA ROBIN LARCHER
&
SILO COUNTRY
please visit:

Email: larcherobin@gmail.com
Twitter: twitter.com/RobinLarcher
Facebook: www.facebook.com/amanda.robinlarcher

For more information about
AMBASSADOR INTERNATIONAL
please visit:

www.ambassador-international.com
@AmbassadorIntl
www.facebook.com/AmbassadorIntl